Case Studies in Marriage and Family Therapy

Second Edition

Larry B. Golden
The University of Texas
at San Antonio

PEARSON

Merrill
Prentice Hall

Upper Saddle River, New Jersey
Columbus, Ohio

I dedicate this book to Trudy and Herb Schurowitz, who have created such a lovely late-in-life marriage.

Library of Congress Cataloging in Publication Data

Golden, Larry B.
  Case studies in marriage and family therapy / Larry B. Golden.— 2nd ed.
     p. cm.
  Includes index.
  ISBN 0-13-098217-2
  1. Family psychotherapy—Case studies. 2. Marital psychotherapy—Case studies.
  I. Title.
  RC488.5.G635 2004
  616.89'156—dc21

2003049829

Vice President and Executive Publisher: Jeffery W. Johnston
Publisher: Kevin M. Davis
Editorial Assistant: Autumn Crisp
Production Editor: Mary Harlan
Production Coordinator: Karen Kennedy, Lithokraft
Design Coordinator: Diane Lorenzo
Text Design: Lithokraft
Cover Design: Ali Mohrman
Cover Image: SuperStock
Production Manager: Laura Messerly
Director of Marketing: Ann Castel Davis
Marketing Manager: Amy June
Marketing Coordinator: Tyra Poole

This book was set in Garamond by Lithokraft. It was printed and bound by R. R. Donnelley & Sons Company. The cover was printed by Phoenix Color Corp.

Pearson Education Ltd.
Pearson Education Singapore Pte. Ltd.
Pearson Education Canada, Ltd.
Pearson Education–Japan

Pearson Education Australia Pty. Limited
Pearson Education North Asia Ltd.
Pearson Educación de Mexico, S.A. de C.V.
Pearson Education Malaysia Pte. Ltd

10 9 8 7 6 5 4 3 2
ISBN: 0-13-098217-2

Foreword

It doesn't much signify whom one marries, for one is sure to find out next morning that it was someone else.

Samuel Rogers

Is Marriage and Family Therapy (MFT) a philosophy or a tool? Is it a way of practice or a way of life? Regardless, marriage and family therapists are in the business of reducing the misery that families and couples have created for themselves.

As practitioners we study philosophy, theory, and ethics. But at the heart of practice is the way that we use ourselves to impact the lives of others. Casebooks describe the myriad ways that competent professionals practice. The search for the best, perfect, right, or correct approach is over. As professionals we need to learn to be good enough to make a positive difference in the lives of others. Good enough to realize that there are many possible ways to help others.

By reading the varied ways of helping in this volume, it is possible to come up with novel ideas that you can use in your practice of marriage and family therapy. The editor and his contributors have provided some very interesting and creative examples of how to work with some of the most common and challenging situations families face.

In my foreword to the first edition, I stated that, "Counselors-in-training, regardless of their enthusiasm, must initially learn from the experience of others before being granted permission or license to practice independently." As you read this volume, notice what you can use and what might be helpful for families. Leave your critical lens off and search for what you can take from this excellent collection of cases.

Jon Carlson
Governors State University

Jon Carlson, Psy.D., Ed.D., is a professor of psychology and counseling at Governors State University (Illinois) and practices psychology at the Lake Geneva Wellness Clinic in Wisconsin. Jon is the founding editor of *The Family Journal: Counseling and Therapy for Couples and Families*, and he has written 30 books and 130 journal articles and developed 150 professional videotapes. Jon is past president of the International Association of Marriage and Family Counselors.

Preface

For this, the second edition, I have three new contributors. Montserrat Casado tells the story of an immigrant family, and Bibiana Gutierrez introduces us to a lesbian relationship. Albert Valadez's case is noteworthy for its powerful use of metaphor.

I have a word about the state of practice, especially my own 25-year practice. In the years since I started in the glory fee-for-service days of the late 1970s, the working environment of counselors has been transformed by harsh economic conditions. The number of outpatient sessions and the length-of-stay of patients in psychiatric hospitals have declined, as have private practice fees.

I think that marriage and family therapy is adapting successfully in the marketplace because it is inherently cost-efficient. When you treat the system, you get results. For me efficient therapy doesn't specify a particular counseling approach (although there are certain methods, notably cognitive-behavior therapy, that are supported by efficacy research). Instead, efficient therapy is characterized by a particular bias: the counselor provides the minimum assistance necessary to alleviate the presenting symptoms.

I like to use the term "time-efficient" rather than "brief" when discussing contemporary approaches to therapy. In short, what I mean is that just because a particular case requires many sessions does not mean that it is inefficient. For example, my own case, *The Boy Who Wouldn't Leave Home*, is ongoing after 15 years and more than 250 sessions. When readers consider the context, they may agree with me that this was an efficient use of therapeutic time.

The very idiosyncrasy that makes case studies interesting can thwart attempts to compare and contrast one case with another, but I've tried to solve this problem the way I try to solve most problems: organization. There's the *Summary of Cases* on page x, a chart that categorizes the 19 studies in terms of "Identified Patient and Presenting Problem," "Systemic Foci," and "Featured Strategies." For example, Phyllis Erdman's identified patient is a 17-year-old boy with a presenting problem of substance abuse. However, her systemic focus is an extramarital affair. She uses emotionally focused therapy and a reflecting team as therapeutic strategies.

Each of the cases follows the same format. I introduce each case and its author. The author's opening paragraphs present background information about the client and therapist. Who are the clients, and why were they referred? What is the presenting problem, and who is the identified patient? What was the practice setting? How were session fees paid? Were there limits on the number of sessions? Each case includes the subsections described next.

- *Conceptualization.* Authors discuss their diagnosis, therapeutic goals, and reasons for choosing specific interventions. I don't push my authors for a DSM-IV-TR diagnosis, given the ongoing (and forever) antagonism between the medical model and the narrative perspective that a formal diagnosis may only contribute to a problem-saturated story!
- *Process.* Authors describe session-by-session client contacts.
- *Outcome.* Therapeutic results may vary from miserable to excellent. In most cases the outcomes are mixed. Such is the case with therapy in the real world.
- *Discussion.* With the benefit of hindsight, how would the authors have done it differently? How have their own marital and family issues influenced their work as therapists?
- *Biographical Statement.* This establishes the author's credentials and provides an e-mail address. All of the authors have told me that they are happy to respond to reader e-mail. My e-mail address is lgolden@utsa.edu. Get in touch!

I think that this book works best as an adjunct to a comprehensive text that presents the major marriage and family therapy theories. What you get here is an honest view of the occasionally brilliant and sometimes slogging work of marriage and family therapists. Please note that, in every case, the identity of clients has been carefully disguised in order to protect confidentiality.

I wish to acknowledge the help I received with proofreading from Rose Balboa, Genesis Wagner, and Dorothy Warren, graduate assistants in our counseling program at UTSA, and expert assistance from production editors Jennifer Murtoff and Marty Sopher, copyeditor Robert Sean Becker, and Publisher Kevin Davis of Merrill/Prentice Hall.

I also want to express my gratitude to the following reviewers for their intelligent and helpful suggestions: Scot Allgood, Utah State University; James A. Holter, University of Wisconsin–Superior; and David Rosenthal, University of Iowa.

Larry B. Golden, Ph.D.
The University of Texas at San Antonio

Discover the Companion Website Accompanying This Book

The Prentice Hall Companion Website: A Virtual Learning Environment
Technology is a constantly growing and changing aspect of our field that is creating a need for content and resources. To address this emerging need, Prentice Hall has developed an online learning environment for students and professors alike—Companion Websites—to support our textbooks.

In creating a Companion Website, our goal is to build on and enhance what the textbook already offers. For this reason, the content for each user-friendly website is organized by topic and provides the professor and student with a variety of meaningful resources. Common features of a Companion Website include:

For the Professor—

Every Companion Website integrates **Syllabus Manager**™, an online syllabus creation and management utility.

- **Syllabus Manager**™ provides you, the instructor, with an easy, step-by-step process to create and revise syllabi, and with direct links into the Companion Website and other online content.

- Students may log on to your syllabus during any study session. All they need to know is the web address for the Companion Website and the password you've assigned to your syllabus.

- After you have created a syllabus using **Syllabus Manager**™, students may enter the syllabus for their course section from any point in the Companion Website.

- By clicking on a date, the student is shown the list of activities for the assignment. The activities for each assignment are linked directly to actual content, saving time for students.

- Adding assignments consists of clicking on the desired due date, then filling in the details of the assignment—name of the assignment, instructions, and whether it is a one-time or repeating assignment.

- In addition, links to other activities can be created easily. If the activity is online, a URL can be entered in the space provided, and it will be linked automatically in the final syllabus.

- Your completed syllabus is hosted on our servers, allowing convenient updates from any computer on the Internet. Changes you make to your syllabus are immediately available to your students at their next log on.

For the Student—

- **Counseling Topics**—17 core counseling topics that represent the diversity and scope of today's counseling field.
- **Annotated Bibliography**—includes seminal foundational works and key current works.
- **Web Destinations**—lists significant and up-to-date practitioner and client sites.
- **Professional Development**—provides helpful information regarding professional organizations and codes of ethics.
- **Electronic Bluebook**—sends homework or essays directly to your instructor's e-mail.
- **Message Board**—serves as a virtual bulletin board to post or respond to questions or comments from a national audience.
- **Chat**—provides real-time chat with anyone who is using the text anywhere in the country. Ideal for discussion and study groups, class projects, etc.

To take advantage of these and other resources, please visit the *Case Studies in Marriage and Family Therapy,* Second Edition, Companion Website at
www.prenhall.com/golden

Contents

Summary of Cases

Case	Identified Patient and Presenting Problem	Systemic Foci	Featured Therapeutic Strategies
1 Angera & Littrell	Married man Addiction to Internet	Extramarital affair	Solution-focused
2 Carey	Boy, age 4 Violent acting out	Problem-saturated family stories	Narrative
3 Casado	Single mother; girl, age 3 Situational depression	Divorce, new relationship, adjustment to new culture	Experiential, Play/filial, Multicultural
4 Conoley	Boy, age 14 School avoidance, depression	Scapegoating of family members	Milan systemic
5 Erdmann	Boy, age 17 Substance abuse	Extramarital affair	Emotionally focused, Reflecting team
6 Evans	Married woman Unresolved bereavement	Family-of-origin, marital communication	Adlerian, Cognitive-behavioral
7 Geil & Walsh	Siblings, ages 23, 18, 14, 11 Substance and sexual abuse	Communication in blended families	Solution-focused
8 Gold	Boy, age 10; girl, age 14 Hypersensitivity/Withdrawal	Adolescent separation	Structural, Family scripting
9 Golden	Boy, age 18 Schizophrenia	Enmeshment	Long-term supportive
10 Gutierrez	Woman, age 38 Depression, anxiety	Impact of "coming out" as a lesbian on family relationships	Therapeutic journey
11 Hanna	Boy, age 2 Constipation (psychosomatic)	Marital discord	Strategic, Use of metaphor
12 Jordan	Married couple Poor communication	Cultural differences in marriage	Solution oriented, Multicultural
13 Kane	Married woman Anxiety, insomnia	Family secrets Family-of-origin issues	Family-of-origin, Genogram, Medication
14 Neben	Boy, age 16 Defiance	Cycle of defensiveness in family	MRI Brief Therapy
15 O'Malley	Married couple Emotional distance	Lack of attachment	Psychodynamic
16 Pillari	Married man "Control freak"	Rigid communication	Bowenian
17 Scofield	Married couple Poor communication	Family-of-origin influence on marital communication	Experiential (self-as-instrument), Genogram
18 Sells	Married woman Dissociative Disorder	Marital relationship as healing agent for psychopathology	Object relations
19 Valadez	Married couple Verbal abuse	Rigid but obtuse roles in marriage	Narrative, Communication skills

1

Internet Man

Jeffrey J. Angera and John M. Littrell

Internet addiction and chat room love affairs are attention-grabbing topics, so I was delighted when Angera (the therapist) and Littrell (the supervisor and mentor) proposed this case about a husband and father involved in an Internet relationship. Angera uses brief, solution-focused therapy in an attempt to bring the addictive behavior under control and to repair the damaged marriage and family relationships.

I, Jeff Angera, am a neophyte therapist growing up professionally in the managed-care era. My training in marriage and family therapy includes a strong systemic emphasis. I have studied the foundational approaches to marriage and family therapy and incorporate many ideas from these models into my clinical work. However, I am also aware that my clinical style has been considerably influenced by prevailing trends in mental health. Managed care dictates that clinicians demonstrate observable, measurable change in a relatively short period of time. Consequently, the therapeutic model I have found most useful in many clinical situations is brief, solution-focused therapy.

This approach proved to be a versatile and pragmatic tool in working with Irv, a 400-pound male in his mid-40s. Irv was severely depressed, and his pastor had encouraged him to see a therapist. Irv's family was on the verge of leaving. His wife, Sara, had filed for divorce because of Irv's "affair" with the Internet. Sara had given Irv a deadline of one month to get help or she would force him to move out and finalize the divorce.

The precipitating event for the depression and withdrawal from his family had begun six months before the appointment, when Irv started using the Internet and the chat rooms. Now Irv fantasized suicide in a car crash. I probed in considerable depth and determined that Irv was not actively suicidal.

Irv was so obsessive in his Internet use that he was spending most waking moments on-line. Irv had accrued a credit card debt of more than $4,000 paying phone bills and access fees for Internet service. He was no longer working as a self-employed plumber.

When Irv was referred to me after a psychiatric examination, I was a staff therapist at a county hospital in a midsize midwestern city. The majority of my clients didn't have much money. Typically, clients received services paid for and managed by the county or state. Because Irv's financial condition had significantly deteriorated due to his preoccupation with the Internet and subsequet avoidance of work, he was receiving government assistance. I was authorized to conduct a maximum of 10 sessions before having to file an appeal for more.

Conceptualization

DSM-IV-TR Diagnosis. Irv met with a psychiatrist a week before our first appointment. This evaluation resulted in the following five-axis diagnosis:

AXIS I:	Major depressive disorder, single episode, moderate
AXIS II:	Obsessive–compulsive personality traits
AXIS III:	No acute illness; extreme obesity
AXIS IV:	Marital discord with possible divorce
AXIS V:	Global Assessment of Functioning 55–60

The psychiatrist's stated goal was to reduce depressive symptoms and enhance coping skills. He prescribed Serazone, an antidepressant. Irv took this prescription for two weeks and then discontinued its use because he did not like the side effects. Irv believed he could manage his depression without medication.

Goals and Strategies. Many of the tenets of solution-focused therapy challenge traditional problem-focused therapy models and the usefulness of DSM-IV-TR diagnoses. Primarily as a result of taking seminars from my coauthor, John Littrell, I have adopted solution-focused therapy as my major counseling modality. According to Littrell (1998), solution-focused counseling is:

1. relationship-based and rests on a foundation of facilitative conditions.
2. time-limited.
3. practical and future-oriented.
4. action-based, giving clients tasks to perform.
5. socially interactive.
6. specific and concrete versus abstract.
7. attentive to typical developmental concerns.
8. humorous and fun.

When I approach a new case, I look for client resources, motivation for change, and observable goals that can serve as markers for the client's progress. In some instances solution-focused therapy is not appropriate, but for Irv there appeared to be a good fit between his present problems and the solution-focused approach.

I want to discuss the notion of doing marital and family therapy with only one person. Irv's main goal was to "get his family back." However, Irv's wife had little hope and was not interested in joining him in counseling until he addressed his Internet addiction. As a systemic thinker, I reminded myself that the individual sitting before me was a part of an intimate relationship that he wanted to preserve.

You may wonder why weight loss was not a therapeutic goal. The answer is that Irv didn't want this as his goal. I hoped that if the depressive symptoms and relational challenges were addressed, the bingeing behavior would decrease. I eventually referred Irv to our hospital's staff dietitians, who provided nutritional education.

Process

Session 1. As in all of my cases, I began by building a therapeutic relationship. Rapport was not easy to achieve. Irv appeared shy, avoided eye contact, and spoke with a nervous, pressured speech. I suspected bipolar tendencies. Irv went off on tangents, so I spent considerable time refocusing on relevant topics. I usually have a good sense if I am connecting, but with Irv I was uncertain. Though he spoke incessantly, he did not provide social cues to indicate he was tracking our conversation.

In our county mental health system, each client first meets with an intake specialist and then is referred to the appropriate service and level of care (e.g., inpatient, partial hospitalization, outpatient, psychiatric evaluation).

Therapist:	I know you've talked to an intake worker, but I want to hear it straight from you. What brings you into therapy, Irv?
Irv:	I just hit bottom! My wife is going to leave me if I don't get help.

Irv described how he had spent the last six months becoming engrossed with the Internet. At the outset, Irv would surf the Internet for information. He soon discovered chat rooms and was instantly consumed with this novel way to communicate. Irv made "friends" in chat rooms and progressed to the point of being on the Internet almost every waking moment. When he wasn't online he was thinking about it. He skipped plumbing jobs and was on the brink of financial ruin.

After gathering a brief description of the problem, I explored Irv's primary motivation for change. From my solution-oriented perspective, I never assume I understand the reasons that a client may want to change.

Therapist:	I am curious. What about this situation is most troubling for you?
Irv:	(resoundingly) I'm going to lose my family. I knew things were bad, but last week my wife told me to get out. I realized I was going to lose everything.

Next, I asked Irv about his previous attempts to deal with the problem. In fact, Irv's wife had initiated most of the attempted solutions. She had reached out to him by encouraging him to go to church, starting conversations, and trying to include him in family events. These attempts proved futile. Exasperated, she had filed for divorce 45 days before our first session. Irv still wasn't sufficiently motivated. Finally, his wife gave him two weeks' notice to leave the house. It took another week for him to hit bottom and, in a panic, try to change his situation.

Therapist:	(pause) Once you resolved to change, what did you try first?
Irv:	I went to my pastor and asked her for help. She had asked me to stop coming to church several months ago because I was disrupting the service by crying. I used to sing in the choir but I couldn't do that without crying. My pastor said she would talk to my wife to see if she would give me a second chance if I agreed to come here and see you for professional help. My wife went along with it as long as I continued with therapy. So that's how I got here.

I asked about exceptions to Irv's problem times. I wanted to learn how his new mobilization influenced his depressive symptoms. Irv's demeanor turned more positive as he described how, since he had hit bottom and made the decision to get help, his crying spells had decreased and his sleeping pattern had become more regular. He also described a slight improvement in his relationships with his wife and his youngest daughter, who still lived at home (she had also rejected him but was speaking to him again since his agreement to seek help).

To top off his difficulties, Irv had gained more than 100 pounds in the past year. He was now an extremely obese man who could not fit into my office chairs. He labored miserably when walking or attempting to sit down. Irv reported constantly eating large quantities of unhealthful foods.

As a novice therapist, I can easily feel overwhelmed by the complexity of clients' presenting problems. I felt this way with Irv. However, I found solace in the assumption of solution-focused therapy that complex problems don't necessarily require complex solutions. I took a deep breath and remembered to start by using the expertise of the client to lead the search for solutions. Irv had already begun to change, and he was motivated (although the motivation was sparked by his wife).

Therapist:	Irv, we've talked about a lot of things that are difficult for you right now. How will we know when we have addressed everything we need to in counseling and you are moving in the right direction?
Irv:	That's easy. I'll be back with my family.
Therapist:	What will you be doing when you are back with your family? What will your wife see you doing?
Irv:	I will be spending more time with them.
Therapist:	And what types of activities will you be doing?

Here, I was moving toward greater specificity and more observable goals.

Irv:	I will be paying more attention to my wife, like sitting with her to watch TV, picking her up from work, and holding hands with her.

Irv became aware that positive change was gathering momentum. I wanted him to see that he was in control of the desired behavior. Before ending our first session, I assigned a homework task based on the goals generated during our session. I asked Irv to go home and make a list of anything he was doing differently since he had made the decision to get help. This task was solution-focused, action-based, and detail-oriented.

In wrapping up, I complimented Irv on his motivation and noticing how his life had changed already since he had set his mind to getting back with his family. Although the session seemed to go well, I didn't feel we had established a sufficient working relationship. I believed that Irv was still seriously depressed. I had plans for a two-week vacation beginning on Monday of the following week. As a precaution, I scheduled another appointment with Irv before leaving.

Session 2. I was afraid that Irv would not return, given the lack of connection I felt. I was pleasantly surprised on Friday morning to see him lumber in. We exchanged greetings, and Irv immediately stated he had completed Monday's homework assignment. He proudly handed me his computer-generated list of changes, which was organized into two columns. One was labeled, "What I was doing before," and the other, "Now, what I'm doing differently." Irv had done an honest job of listing the various behaviors that had gotten him into trouble: too much time on the Internet, watching TV, eating, avoiding his family and his job. His new and desirable behaviors included cold-turkey withdrawal from the Internet, a reduction in TV watching and overeating, more communication with his wife and family, and restarting his plumbing business.

Before we reviewed the list, I again attended to relationship building. I have had instances when I have enthusiastically rushed into goal setting only to find the person drops out because, I hypothesize, I had not adequately laid the relationship groundwork. In my opinion, this is a pitfall of solution-oriented therapy that can be avoided if therapists take care to understand the client's conception of the problem before implementing solution-focused tasks.

I took the time to really listen to Irv. I wanted him to know that I was there for him. In addition, I reemphasized the safe, confidential nature of therapy. Aside from legal responsibilities to inform, I would not tell his wife, pastor, kids, or anybody else anything that he said. This second reminder made a difference. Two subtle but observable indicators of his increased comfort included a marginal increase in eye contact and less pressured speech.

As Irv's comfort in our session increased, he disclosed more specifics. On the Internet, Irv, in addition to being himself, assumed three other distinct personas. As himself, Irv used accurate identifiers, including reference to his weight problems. He described himself as "relatively heavy set."

Irv's first false persona was Tom, an average guy who was divorced, shy, and "nothing too special." A second persona was Jaime, an affluent Latin American male who managed an upscale restaurant. Jaime was a debonair ladies' man. Irv's third persona was "Sweet Sara," an attractive woman in her mid-30s. Sweet Sara was a bored housewife with three children, looking for excitement. Sara flirted and enticed men (you may recall that Irv's wife is named Sara).

As Irv described the false personas he became animated. He enjoyed the ability to experiment with being someone else. Though a bit embarrassed in detailing his Internet life, Irv was relieved to share the burden of this clandestine life with me. His motivation in setting up the personas was to discover how others would react to different scenarios. For example, if Irv was talking to a woman or group of women as himself, he would also simultaneously log in to the chat room as his persona Jaime, so as to gauge women's responses. Irv reported that invariably these women made excuses about why they had to sign off with him (Irv) only to engage the mythical Jaime.

I reframed Irv's Internet behavior as his attempt to build relationships without fear of rejection due to his weight, appearance, or shyness. This reframe fit quite well and elicited accounts of his activities that went beyond the Internet. Irv had actually met some of the women with whom he had chatted. The majority of the contacts were with one woman, Gloria, who lived 200 miles away. Irv (as himself) arranged to meet Gloria at a public park in her hometown. After that, Irv and Gloria's five or so meetings involved going to dinner, returning to her home, and watching movies. He admitted that they hugged and kissed but maintained it never went beyond that. Irv put an end to the relationship when his wife, Sara, filed for divorce. Irv declared that he could never tell Sara about Gloria.

Therapist:	It seems to me that you were trying to develop safe relationships and find companionship.
Irv:	Yeah, and the funny thing is that all of that was right under my nose in my own family.
Therapist:	I'm impressed with your wisdom to recognize this. Now it's just a matter of following through on your list in the hope of regaining what you had all along.

Irv told me about other obsessive behaviors, from taping thousands of movies after purchasing his first VCR to collecting anything related to Harley-Davidson motorcycles. Irv also told me about the physical and emotional abuse his parents had inflicted. I listened attentively and acknowledged these points and then redirected him to his list.

I complimented Irv on the strength it must have taken to overcome those historical difficulties. From a solution-focused perspective, it was important to genuinely listen to these multiproblem descriptions or rationalizations for behaviors but not to get trapped in their complexity. Though these historical antecedents were very real, Irv had successfully developed interventions that he believed could improve relationships with his current family and, consequently, alleviate his depression. As a clinician, I could have easily labeled Irv with numerous diagnoses (e.g., major depression, dysthymia, obsessive–compulsive personality, eating disorder, and mania), but these labels would have done little to change or alter his current situation. Rather, by relying on the progress he had already initiated and his desire to change, I helped Irv focus on new ways of behaving.

Because I was going to be vacationing for two weeks, we discussed how he would remind himself to continue taking positive strides. My coauthor, John Littrell, emphasizes the need for people to have visual cues to remind them of their goals. Without such cues, the tasks often fade from awareness as daily events take precedence. So when Irv said he would "just remember" his list, I asked if there was any place he could put it to ensure that he observed it daily. Because he spent many hours in his home business office that was solely "his" space, we agreed that he would tape the list to his computer. I hoped that this strategy would remind Irv to avoid the Internet. We agreed to meet for a third session in two weeks.

Session 3. At the beginning of the session, I asked Irv to discuss the positive progress he had made on his list. I made the assumption that positive change had occurred.

Therapist:	Tell me how you've progressed on your list.
Irv:	(very animated) I'm going to bed around 10 o'clock and pretty much sleeping through the night, only waking up once or twice. I'm also starting to work again. I have two half-day jobs set up for this week. It ain't great, but it's a start. I'm also eating more normally. I went to see that dietitian you told me about. I also went back to church, and I wasn't crying at all. And best of all, I'm getting along a lot better with my family. My wife had to get a job to help us make ends meet. Well, I've been picking her up after work. Also, we go grocery shopping together. I haven't done that with her in almost 20 years! It's like new territory in my life. (Irv wore a big smile.)
Therapist:	Wow! You went to work.

I extensively complimented Irv and stressed that "new territory" can be untamed. To emphasize Irv's relationships, I asked him whether significant people in his life were noticing his changes. He said his daughters and wife had commented on how much more social and loving he had become. We spent the remainder of the session discussing the various new behaviors on his list, how well his family had responded, and how much better he now felt.

We planned to meet in three weeks for a final checkup session. Again, I instructed him to attend to what he was doing differently, and more specifically, to observe how this new behavior was influencing other people.

Final Session. Irv had lost 12 pounds by eating in accord with the dietitian's directives and by refraining from bingeing. Relationships with his family continued to improve. Seeking observable changes, I asked him to give me examples. One instance involved a change in the dinner ritual. In the past, Irv would fill his plate with food and retreat to the den to watch television, leaving his wife and youngest daughter at the table. Now he was either sitting at the table conversing with his family or joining them in the den to eat together and watch television.

Irv was also taking control of impulsive buying habits.

Irv: In the past, I would throw something in my shopping cart without giving it a second thought. But this time I thought to myself, "We just don't have the money for this now, and we really don't need it yet, so I'll wait until later." And you know, I didn't give it another thought, I just ditched it.

Irv provided one last example regarding the family's debts. Sara had assumed responsibility for paying the bills. Now his wife was happy to have Irv resume this chore, a tangible indicator that he was earning his wife's trust.

Over the course of our sessions, I saw increased eye contact. By this final session, Irv was making eye contact regularly. After I commented on this behavioral indicator of change, he laughed and relished his progress.

Irv: (jokingly) I can finally say I know the color of my counselor's eyes.

We terminated therapy and agreed to leave the option open for future sessions.

■ Outcome

I called Irv six months after our last session. Irv didn't remember my name (definitely not an ego boost), but he remembered after I described my position. I explained that my call was a "six-month checkup."

I asked Irv about each of the subgoals on his list. He said he was not nearly as irritable with his family and was not shutting them out. He was spending only a few hours a day alone. Also, he had not been on the Internet since before our sessions began. Business had picked up considerably, and he was booked one month in advance. Irv had sold most of his tools to support his Internet habit, and he now had to replace them to perform his job effectively. Consequently, the family had incurred a new start-up debt on top of prior debt.

Irv's television viewing was moderate and mostly occurred with family. His sleeping was regular and uninterrupted. Amazingly, Irv had lost 50 pounds with a significant decrease in binge eating.

| Therapist: | How are your relationships with your wife and children? |
| Irv: | A 100% turn-around! |

I asked Irv how therapy had affected him. He indicated that having a confidential place to "get everything out in the open" was most important. He needed someone he could talk to and trust.

▉ Discussion

This case reinforced several tenets of solution-focused therapy. Irv demonstrated that clients often have the resources to solve their problems if we professionals provide the context and facilitative conditions. I had the good fortune to intervene at a point when Irv was motivated. I helped him translate goals into actions that would demonstrate that change was, in fact, occurring.

Although I conceptualized this case as primarily a systemic problem, I saw Irv individually. As I mentioned earlier, I am sometimes overwhelmed by the complexity of the problems that people present. This often results in "brief therapeutic panic," in which I struggle to maintain a systemic view. If I were presented with Irv's case again, I would get his family into my office. From Irv's reports, all his family members—particularly his wife—were invested in his getting his life back in order. It may have helped to involve these people in the therapeutic process in order to develop a feedback loop to help Irv recognize the impact of his behavior. Further, this involvement may have reinforced to the family that Irv acknowledged the seriousness of the situation.

I was pleased with my ability to stay solution-focused despite Irv's intriguing information about his various personas. I was tempted to explore Irv's fascinating personas in detail and thereby become stuck in problem-saturated mud. As it was, I stayed the solution-focused course and continued to emphasize what worked in Irv's world.

I recognize that, from some theoretical perspectives, Irv's termination from therapy would be viewed as premature because psychological issues remained. From a brief, solution-focused perspective, however, the timing of Irv's termination was appropriate. Irv entered therapy unable to function effectively at work or in his family relationships. In four sessions he was back on track developmentally. If there is no presenting problem, there is no need for therapy.

My own family of origin was middle-class, and it was there that I learned the values of hard work and caring for family. In my professional life, I assume that hard work is a given; in my personal life, my marriage is my highest priority. I sensed that Irv and I shared the two values of hard work and caring for family but that he had lost his bearings on the Internet. The search for solutions in Irv's life was facilitated by my assessment and my strong belief that Irv possessed in his repertoire the skills, knowledge, and determination to find his way again. Irv entered therapy as Internet Man. Therapy ended because Irv was able once more to resume his place as Family Man.

One last thought—I think therapists can expect to see more relationship problems associated with using the Internet. Lonely people engage others on the Internet only to find themselves increasingly isolated (Sleek, 1998; Sanders et al., 2000).

References

Littrell, J. M. (1998). *Brief counseling in action*. New York: W. W. Norton.

Sanders, C. E., Field, T. M., Diego, M., and Chaplain, M. (2000). The relationship of Internet use to depression and social isolation among adolescents. *Adolescence, 35* (138), 237–242.

Sleek, S. (1998, September). Isolation increases with Internet use. *APA Monitor, 29* (1), 30–31.

Biographical Statement

Jeffrey J. Angera, Ph.D., is an assistant professor of human development and family studies at Central Michigan University. He is a licensed marriage and family therapist in Michigan. Jeff and John Littrell coauthored "A Solution-Oriented Approach in Couple and Family Counseling," which can be found in *Social Construction in Couple and Family Counseling* by J. D. West, D. L. Bubenzer, & J. R. Bitter, 1998. You can reach Jeff at jeffrey.j.angera@cmich.edu

John M. Littrell, Ed.D., is professor and program coordinator of counselor education at Iowa State University. He has presented national workshops for the American Counseling Association on the topic of brief counseling. His book *Brief Counseling in Action* (1998) and its accompanying videotapes are published by W. W. Norton. You can reach John at jlittrel@iastate.edu.

2

<u>When the Problem Becomes a Gift</u>

<u>Gabrielle Carey</u>

We meet Gabrielle Carey during her training program. She is an idealistic and energetic family therapist. Andy was referred to her when his weary mother and worried school authorities had become convinced of a need for an individual assessment for brain damage or psychopathology. Such a problem-saturated perspective bodes ill for successful therapy, but Carey helps the family create a more hopeful narrative.

Andy, 4 years old, was referred about halfway through my marriage and family therapy internship. Andy's mother wanted him evaluated before entering kindergarten. She and teachers at Andy's preschool had observed wild, violent behavior and suspected that there might be brain damage or some sort of psychopathology. Andy's pediatrician suggested Andy and his mother see a family counselor before referring the child to a pediatric neurologist.

Although I had taken two child assessment classes, I was nervous about this case. I was in one of my occasional professional slumps. While my internship was a great learning experience and sometimes I thought I was destined to be a great therapist, at other times I felt like a great impostor.

My internship site was a brand-new project. The school district rented space in a shopping mall for use as a family counseling center. Our clients were referred by school counselors, and most of our families were at low- to middle-income levels and could not afford to see private practitioners. Our standard fee was $25 per session, but this was negotiable. We hoped that the program would expand by word of mouth.

We shared space with volunteer tutors who gave lessons in English as a second language and basic high school subjects. The volunteers were a little fussy about having toys and crayons all over the place, so I could not encourage children to be active and free with their choice of play.

Conceptualization

With neatness in mind, I surveyed the counseling office.

"If this child misbehaves and acts violently, I had better childproof this room," I thought, while putting everything breakable in drawers. I hid the tempera paints and the clay in the cupboards. I left only the washable markers and a large pad of paper within reach.

So much for nondirective play therapy. My approach to family therapy was in the early stages. In my graduate program, we were introduced to all the theories in marriage and family therapy and then encouraged to concentrate on one approach during each semester of our internship. In my first semester I attempted a "brief strategic" approach similar to that of Jay Haley, Cloe Madanes, and the Milan group. Now, in my second semester, my chosen approach was "narrative."

Narrative therapy is about listening to the stories families tell. Each person has a different perspective, and each perspective is honored equally. I expected to listen to Andy's parents' stories and, through play therapy, come to understand his own narrative. In therapy, narratives are more than just words, they are tales of meaning. People share their stories with verbal and nonverbal forms of communication. I hoped to be able to help the family change their problem-saturated stories and create more positive alternatives.

The original problem story was that Andy was a destructive, disobedient, "very disturbed" little boy. This story contrasted with my impressions of mother and son.

Before becoming a therapist, I had been a middle school teacher. I was the mother of two daughters and the eldest of a vast number of first cousins. Andy did not seem out of the ordinary, let alone a wild, uncontrollable child.

Although I was using a narrative approach, I was integrating it with my former approach of brief strategic therapy. In strategic approaches, the therapist begins with a hypothesis about the case and reassesses it during the session. My original hypothesis, that Andy was abnormal, was immediately put into question. I began to listen closely to Jeanette's tales of Andy's exploits. What were the exceptions to Andy's destructive behaviors? What else was going on in the environment? What other possibilities could explain Jeanette's frustration?

Each session brought new hypotheses and new possibilities into view. The family narrative became rich with description and detail. Jeanette was newly wed and seven months pregnant. She was working part-time in a daycare facility while raising an active, intelligent four-year-old. It was easy to see how Jeanette could feel "stressed-out."

Narrative family therapy involves continual assessment and questioning of goals while gathering each participant's perceptions. Jeanette needed help with parenting and more rest. Stanley, in his new role as stepfather, was unclear about what he could do to help Jeanette and how to deal with Andy. Andy needed more attention.

The original problem story about Andy as a very disturbed child frightened his parents to the point that it became an insurmountable obstacle in their new married life. By normalizing Andy's upsetting behavior as merely attention-seeking by an intelligent and active child, Stanley was able to embrace his role as stepfather. Everyone relaxed and things began to flow smoothly. Although therapy had been brief, it was enough to get this family through a difficult adjustment. In leaving therapy with a positive outcome, they would likely seek therapy again if necessary.

■ Process

Session 1. Mother and son arrived promptly. Jeanette was a tall, thin woman with pale skin and light brown hair worn in a tightly curled perm. She was obviously six or seven months pregnant and exhausted. She acknowledged my greeting and then glanced down.

Jeanette: This is my son, Andy.
Therapist: (Stooping down, I shook his hand.) Hi, Andy.

Andy was adorable and was dressed tastefully. His sandy hair, straight and glossy, was cut in a bowl shape. His bright eyes were full of sprightly mischief, which reminded me of the "Little Rascal" Spanky. He was also *very* active.

He politely answered my questions and readily offered all sorts of additional information. I was a bit shocked by his articulate speech. Actually, I was shocked by my whole first impression. I had expectations of meeting a child of lower intelligence, not much verbal ability, no manners, and incorrigible, outrageous behaviors. I wondered, "Do I have the right family?"

Therapist: Andy, would you draw a picture of your family while I talk to your
               mother?

In one swift movement Andy was up and over to the shelf where I had placed the markers. Holding the box over his head, he jumped for joy.

Andy: With these markers?
Therapist: Sure, let me give you a piece of paper and get you set up on the
               floor.
Jeanette: (becoming noticeably agitated) Remember, those are new clothes
               and we are going to Stanley's parents' house for dinner tonight.

Jeanette proceeded to document numerous incidents of messes, tantrums, sassy behaviors, and limit testing that Andy had perpetrated.

Therapist: It must be extremely hard to be pregnant at the same time you are
               working and raising a very active 4-year-old! How do you do it?
Jeanette: (sighing, in a rueful tone) It's not easy! But Stanley helps.
Therapist: Who is Stanley?
Jeanette: Stanley is my new husband. We got married after this baby was con-
               ceived. I told him that he didn't have to marry me, but he convinced
               me that he really wanted to. We had been dating for a year, ever since
               he graduated from college and moved back to San Antonio. Stanley
               was friends with my ex-husband's younger brother; that's how we
               met. My ex's family lives in town, but my ex moved to Kansas. He al-
               most never calls, except for Andy's birthdays.

Jeanette's voice became louder as she criticized her ex-husband. Andy paused, marker in midair, and listened intently. I tilted my head and looked at Andy quizzically.

Therapist: Your dad calls you on your birthday?
Andy: (proudly) Yup. He gave me a mighty, triple, hook-and-ladder fire
               truck, too.
Jeanette: A toy fire engine. Andy wants to be a fireman when he grows up.

Talk about problem saturated stories! Jeanette documented how Andy misbehaved and the various ways that his dad was irresponsible. I picked up on the exception, Dad's birthday gifts and calls. Also, instead of talking to Jeanette as if Andy were not in the room, I used circular questioning to redirect her comments to him.

Therapist: Do you want to be a fireman when you grow up?
Andy: (intently concentrating on his drawing) Maybe. He never plays with
               me.
Therapist: Who, your dad?
Andy: No, Stanley.
Jeanette: (quickly admonishing) That is simply not true, Andy! We have had
               some trouble with fibbing.

While Andy began to draw with longer and darker strokes, Jeanette explained how Stanley spent time with Andy on weekends. During the week, Stanley came home late at night and Andy was already in bed.

Jeanette:	If you would clean up your room you would have more play time.
Andy:	You take my toys away.
Jeanette:	Because you don't put them away. You'll get them back as soon as you learn to keep your room neat.
Therapist:	Have you lost many toys, Andy?
Andy:	All of them. Except my teddy and blankey.

I slipped down to the floor beside Andy.

Therapist:	What are you drawing?
Andy:	You know. . . .
Therapist:	Is that your pet?
Andy:	(giggling) No.
Therapist:	(teasing) Is it a huge, scaly dinosaur?
Andy:	No, it's Puff.
Therapist:	Putt who?
Andy:	PUFF! (giggling, before bursting into a shrill soprano) You know, Puff the magic dragon lived by the sea and froglipped in the ocean mist in a land called Hannah-lee. . . .
Therapist:	I sang that song when I was in school. (looks to Jeanette) Do you know that song?
Jeanette:	Yes, Andy plays the tape all the time! It's his favorite.

Jeanette and I joined in as Andy sang. I could only hum, having forgotten the words, but Jeanette knew every word. We were soon laughing and joking. The mood of the session had changed, for which I was grateful, because our time was almost up.

Therapist:	Where's your family, Andy? I thought I asked you to draw your family, you silly!
Andy:	(pointing to a small black stick figure in the lower right corner of the drawing) Here's me!

Session 2. Jeanette immediately began telling me about how Andy had been naughty, creating messes and disturbances. She described his punishments and his reactions. Her desperation intensified as she gave me the running account. Out of the corner of my eye I saw Andy snake one of his arms into his T-shirt. I tried to interrupt:

Therapist: You must have been at your wit's end, but . . .

Jeanette had too much to say and kept on.

Therapist:	Jeanette, I had asked you to notice when he did clean his room.
Jeanette:	Well, he never did. It has been a very bad week!

By sausaging and squirming, Andy managed to pull his other arm into his T-shirt. I guessed that he was uncomfortable with his mother's stories.

Jeanette: It is as if he is doing it on purpose. I spent the morning cleaning the garage and Andy helped me. He knew he was not supposed to make messes, but when I lay down for a nap, he and the little neighbor girl went in there and spread dirt from my potted plants all over the garage floor.

Andy had managed to get his head into his T-shirt as well as both of his arms. He was a little ball of T-shirt. I thought, "That is one way to escape, like an ostrich hiding its head in the sand or a turtle retreating into its shell. Yes, he even looks like a turtle." Jeanette followed my glance and her eyes widened in disgust.

Jeanette: Andy, what do you think you are doing? Look at me when I am speaking to you.

Andy's head popped out with a grin on his face, but Jeanette was not amused.

Jeanette: You will stretch that shirt out of shape. Take your arms out, right now!
Therapist: Oh there he is! I was wondering where you were, Andy.

I was struck by an image of shame when Andy had pulled his turtle act. Reaching up to my puppet shelf, I took down the turtle puppet.

Therapist: Andy, do you know what a turtle does when it gets scared?
Andy: (Reaching for the turtle puppet, he pulled its head into its shell.) He goes like this! And when he feels happy he comes out again. (He waved the puppet in his mother's face and then in mine, giggling.)
Therapist: What does the turtle think about when he is in his shell?
Andy: He feels bad.
Therapist: Do you ever feel like a turtle in a shell?
Andy: Yes.
Therapist: (speaking directly to the puppet) You know, Mr. Turtle, I think you want to be a good boy who cleans up his own messes. I know you can do it, Mr. Turtle, so I'm going to let you and Andy play with my blocks. I can't wait until it's time to clean up. Then I'll get to see what you can do.

I sat down at the table with Jeanette while Andy started building. I told her that I didn't think his messiness was unusual compared with that of other 4-year-olds.

Therapist: I remember a time when I was about 5 years old. It was rainy, and my sister and I had to play indoors. My mother was furious about the mess we made. She broke the spell that I had been under while we were playing by insisting we clean the room before dinner. I didn't know where to begin or how to clean up such a mess. When my mother came back she found two girls crying in the midst of the disaster. Although she was still angry, she began to teach us how to put our toys away.

Jeanette: Andy has shelves and boxes to store his toys, but he just puts everything under his bed. Lately, I have been very tired. It's not easy working full-time, coming home to cook dinner—and pregnancy is draining me. I just have to depend on Andy to help me by keeping his toys picked up!

Therapist: You are a supermom, but you're not made of steel. Does Stanley ever help or monitor Andy's play?

Jeanette: Not really. Stanley and I are downstairs and Andy plays in his room upstairs.

Therapist: I wonder if Andy is still learning how to clean up his messes. If so, it will be important for you to notice each little step. I think that verbal praise might be all that he needs. (I could see Jeanette's skepticism.) It is like what Andy is doing right now. Andy, what are you building?

Andy: This is a castle. Here's the moat and the towers. I'm still working on it.

Therapist: Andy's castle takes time to build. Each of his good behaviors is like a building block. Over time they will take the shape of a well behaved child.

Jeanette: (smiling and shaking her head) I have my doubts.

Therapist: There are a lot of other things we can try if this does not work. But I have a suspicion that what Andy needs is reinforcement of his positive behaviors. Divorce is so hard on children. They become sad and often blame themselves. This sadness or depression can be expressed in many ways, such as hyperactivity. They can be mistakenly labeled as having attention deficit disorder with hyperactivity. I think Andy is energetic, highly intelligent, and creative, but I am not willing to label him "hyperactive." Would Stanley be willing to come to our sessions to help Andy adjust to your new family?

Jeanette: Yes, I think so, if we can meet after he gets out of work.

Therapist: Good. I have something I want you to try before we meet again. I want you to monitor Andy's play and tell me about every time he cleans up.

Session 3. Stanley was quiet, although not shy. He was an only child of wealthy parents, a clean-cut electrical engineer with a rising career.

Andy and I played with modeling clay as his mom and stepfather told me about Jeanette's difficulty fitting in with Stanley's parents. Jeanette's anxiety about Andy's misbehavior and messiness stemmed, at least in part, from her need to impress her in-laws. She feared that his behavior reflected unflatteringly on her parenting skills.

Stanley: My parents were disappointed that I was dating a divorcée with a child. But when Jeanette told me she was carrying my child, I knew I wanted to marry her.

Jeanette: Stanley's parents don't think I'm good enough for him. They think I trapped him into marrying me.

Stanley: Jeanette, both of my parents have come to like you. We are just not touchy-feely in my family.

Andy asked his parents to play. Jeanette held back and Stanley looked at me for permission. After I encouraged him, he got down on the floor and seemed to enjoy himself.

I asked about Andy's high verbal skills. Jeanette confirmed that this was a strength. I suggested that Andy's behaviors were typical of a highly intelligent, creative child who was bored and needed attention during play.

Therapist: We tend to think of gifted children as problem-free, but it is not unusual for them to develop discipline problems. I suspect that Andy will benefit from more stimulating school-work. Rarely have I met such an articulate 4-year-old.

The anxiety drained away along with the fear that Andy was a damaged, pathological monster. The new frame removed the onus of "bad mother" and Jeanette and Stanley regarded Andy in a new light.

Andy was interlocking the markers one on top of the other. His tower was taller than he was and he had to lay the chain of markers on the floor.

Andy: I did this with Miss Cindy's markers. The tower went all the way up to the roof!
Therapist: Wow! Do you think we can make this one high enough to reach the roof? (No way. The mall ceiling was too high.)
Andy: I'll try.

Andy and Stanley struggled to link the whole chain of 12 markers into one "tower." It was too wobbly and broke when they tried to lift it upright. Jeanette jumped up to assist. The tower pointed up to the ceiling, a wobbly symbol of success. Then, on Andy's cue, they let the tower fall apart. The markers were strewn all over the room. All of us laughed at the mess. Andy, with a little help from Stanley, cleaned up at the end of the session.

Stanley could relate easily to a gifted child, especially as compared with the paralysis he felt when confronted by an emotionally disturbed child.

Sessions 4–7. These sessions continued the mix of play and family therapy and served to reinforce progress and normalize setbacks.

Stanley was coming home from work early so he and Andy could play ball or just watch TV together. When Jeanette went to lie down and rest, Andy would lie down next to her and practice reading. They began to function in tandem, napping together, playing together, and working together. When Andy threw a tantrum or created a mess, his parents handled him as a child who was temporarily out of sorts, but who was expected to come around. Predictably, he did. As Jeanette and Stanley changed their perception of the reason behind his misbehavior, the more manageable Andy became.

The last session took place with Stanley and Andy, as Jeanette was in the hospital with the new family addition, a little girl. It was a quick and pleasant session. While

I realized that the family had sorted its own problems out and had worked hard to improve, I felt as though I might have helped make their goal a reality. Driving home that night, I felt that my perception of my role as a therapist had received a substantial boost. I was doing what I was meant to do.

Outcome

A few weeks later I called Jeanette. Things were going well, although she was exhausted by the demands of an infant. Reportedly, Andy was a help with his little sister. In my judgment, the family had gained confidence in their ability to overcome the inevitable problems that arise in complex relationships. I assured Jeanette that they could always come back for a "booster shot" as needed.

Discussion

I can think of nothing that I would have done differently. I did not plan during the sessions or between the sessions; rather, I let our conversations unfold. My interventions were designed to block the negative stories. In comparing the successful outcome of this case with other cases I considered flops, I realize I have to chalk this success up to beginner's luck and the ability to be flexible enough to use what the clients brought to the session.

I could not have anticipated Andy's turtlelike retreat into his T-shirt, but I was able to use it to redirect therapy to a more positive focus. Luck was with me—I had almost decided on an eagle puppet instead of a turtle!

Andy's marker tower building naturally became a metaphor for building good behaviors and family cooperation, little by little.

In following a narrative approach, I focused on helping the family to create stories, open up alternative views, and obtain different perspectives. I was able to meet with three family members and gain multiple perspectives on the problem. The family's goal had been to find out what was wrong and fix the identified patient. I did not know if Andy was truly a gifted child, and I could not be certain that he was not hyperactive. It was the family's willingness to accept the alternative story that was critical to their success. Once we had defined a workable problem, the solution was set in motion.

Biographical Statement

Gabrielle Carey, Ph.D., is a licensed marriage and family therapist working at the Marriage and Family Institute of San Antonio. She is an American Association of Marriage and Family Therapy Clinical Member and Approved Supervisor. Gabrielle completed a yearlong externship in collaborative language systems at the Houston–Galveston Institute and is a Ph.D. candidate in counseling at St. Mary's University. She is the author of "Competing Voices: A Narrative Intervention" (published in *101 More Interventions in Family Therapy*, Nelson & Trepper, Eds., 1998) and coauthor of a book, *Family Therapy with Hispanics: Toward Appreciating Diversity*. You can reach Gabrielle at CareGab@aol.com.

3

Living Between Two Worlds

Montserrat Casado

Montserrat Casado makes her case for a multicultural perspective, stating that "reactions to the process of adjusting to a new culture, values, and ways of being can be easily mistaken for dysfunction. Although English has been my most frequently used language for the last decade, I still struggle for words to express the intensity of a wide variety of emotions." Like many therapists before her, Casado finds that Carl Rogers and Virginia Satir teach us about the conditions of a truly therapeutic environment. Instead of pathology, Casado looks for resiliency.

My clients are a 36-year-old Hispanic divorced single mother, Graciela, her 3-year-old daughter, Azucena, and Graciela's new boyfriend, 46-year-old Víctor. Graciela is from Chile, and Víctor is from Spain. They are in the United States on an exchange program that has them teaching Spanish in public schools. They met at one of the exchange program's social gatherings.

Graciela was in the United States for only two months prior to seeking counseling. She was referred to me by the counselor at the school where she taught Spanish. The school counselor knew that I was one of the few counselors in the area who provided services in Spanish. Graciela's English was proficient, but she preferred to discuss emotional issues in her native language. Besides, Azucena did not know English. One of the reasons Graciela had decided on the visit to the United States in the first place was to give Azucena an opportunity to learn English.

Graciela complained of feelings of depression and isolation. Graciela also felt guilty about her divorce and wondered about its impact on her daughter. She questioned her ability to raise a well-adjusted child on her own. Graciela felt that Azucena needed a father figure and wondered if she might be tempted to remarry hastily for the sake of Azucena. In Chile, Azucena's beloved grandparents had taken care of her while Graciela worked, but now Azucena was in day care. The day care director was bilingual and had really bonded with Azucena, but the child was still having some adjustment problems. Lately, Azucena had been clinging more to Graciela, and she had been crying and sucking her thumb constantly as well as wetting herself.

When I accepted this case, I was working 20 hours a week at a pastoral counseling agency in a hospital as part of my externship for my doctorate in counselor education. I was also accruing supervised practice hours for licensure as a marriage and family therapist. The agency also served as an educational training setting and was well equipped with a variety of rooms, including a play therapy room. I was seeing a wide variety of clients, including children individually and in group. The agency operated on a sliding scale and served hospital employees as well as the community.

Conceptualization

If I had to provide a diagnosis for Graciela, as the identified patient, I would classify her as having an adjustment disorder with depressed mood. Her sadness, depressive symptoms, crying spells, and feelings of displacement were all related to her moving to a new culture, taking a new job, and maneuvering between two worlds, specifically being Hispanic and adapting to the English-speaking U.S. culture. I believe that her depression was the result of a normal grieving process for all that she had lost. I explored with her the cycle of grief and provided materials about grief as related to the acculturation process.

My therapeutic approach is based on Virginia Satir's experiential family therapy model. Experiential family therapists assume that family dysfunction is a result of suppressed emotions. Therapy focuses on acknowledgement and expression of emotions. Satir (1976) emphasized that congruence, defined as being emotionally honest, is at the heart of making contact. Congruence also involves taking risks. When emotional honesty happens in therapy, healing and transformation occur. Symptoms are seen as efforts for growth, and therapy becomes a safe, nurturing place that fosters hope and promotes intrapersonal change. As an experiential family therapist, my role is that of a facilitator, supporter, and resource person. It is important that I model effective communication skills, be congruent, and make clients aware of their presuppositions and patterns. I believe in the human potential for growth, and I see myself as a change agent.

From an experiential viewpoint, my goals were to (1) allow Graciela to express her feelings and learn how to communicate congruently with Azucena; (2) strengthen the parent-child relationship and reinforce Graciela's parenting skills; (3) redefine symptoms as efforts for growth; (4) establish hope and trust; (5) normalize acculturation issues; and (6) increase Graciela's and Azucena's self-esteem. I also used play therapy and filial therapy to help Graciela strengthen her relationship with Azucena. Play therapy and filial therapy are actually offshoots of experiential therapy and are likewise influenced by Carl Rogers's humanistic approach (Casado, Young, and Rasmus, 2002). In play therapy, the child uses play as a way to communicate. Filial therapy was originally conceptualized by Bernard Guerney as a way to enhance the relationship between parents and children (Landreth, 1991). Filial therapy integrates parents into the play session. Parents learn reflective listening skills by playing with their child in a way that tends to the emotional needs of the child and provides empathy. The use of filial therapy strengthens the bond between parent and child. The use of play therapy was crucial with Azucena since her verbal abilities were limited because of her age. For children her age, play is the primary medium of expression. Developmentally, Azucena did not have the verbal skills to express thoughts and feelings of what was going on in her internal world, but she found ways to act out those feelings. Since cognitive reasoning, verbal abilities, and abstract thinking are not well developed in young children, the use of play in therapy matches the child's appropriate developmental level by providing a concrete experience in which to explore his or her inner emotional world. Thus, play becomes a medium for expressing feelings, developing relationships with others, and creating a sense of self. I believed that the better Graciela felt about herself as an individual, the better she would feel as a mother. I was certain that Graciela was resilient in many ways. It was my role to help her see her many strengths, and those of Azucena's too. Azucena was a very bright child with a very caring spirit. And Graciela had played a major role in Azucena's development despite the many challenges of raising a child as a single parent in a foreign country.

I started family therapy just with Graciela and Azucena, mother and daughter. Later, when Graciela brought in her boyfriend, Víctor, as a potential marriage partner, I moved to couples therapy. The last session focused on blended family issues and included Graciela, Azucena, and Víctor.

▪ Process

The excerpts from various sessions have been provided in English for the reader. In the actual sessions, both English and Spanish were used. At the beginning of treatment, more Spanish was used, particularly with Azucena, who did not speak English. Although Graciela was fluent in English, she did not know how to communicate emotionally laden content in it.

Session 1. Graciela arrived at my office with Azucena. Graciela was feeling quite scared and depressed, but she was also relieved to be able to meet someone in whom she could confide and communicate with in Spanish. Similarities in age and cultural experiences helped us make an immediate connection. I met with both of them in the play therapy room, which allowed me to interact with both of them while observing parent-child interactions as the little girl played. As with all my cases, I began by listening to the client's story. My main goal during the initial session was to make contact and establish a relationship with both mother and daughter while validating their feelings and affirming them as people. I felt trust had been developed and I had sincere empathy for what Graciela was going through as she was trying to adjust with Azucena to a new culture.

Session 2. Graciela came to the session by herself.

Graciela: I fear I have not been a good mother for Azucena. I blame myself for the divorce, even though in my heart I know it was not my fault. I worry that Azucena will grow up messed up. And now, I worry whether I made the right decision in coming to the United States. I thought it would be good for me and Azucena. But now Azucena really misses my mother and family. Although in some ways, I think the move has been good for the two of us. It has allowed us to bond.

Therapist: Graciela, I really hear you struggling with the idea of whether you have been a good mother. Do you think you did the best you could as a mother with what you had going on at the time when Azucena was younger?

Graciela: Yes, I think I did my best but wish I could have done better.

Therapist: Sometimes, we can only do our best, and when we can do differently, we do. I feel like you are very concerned about Azucena's well-being and care for her in many different ways. The strong loving bond between both of you is quite visible. You are a good loving mother, and Azucena is a loving child. That is quite obvious.

Graciela: (She is crying now.) I guess you are right.

Sessions 3-4. Graciela and Azucena attended the sessions together, and we met in the play therapy room. Azucena seemed comfortable and open to engaging us in her play, and this helped Graciela understand Azucena's inner world. At times my role was educational. I shared personal stories of my own process of adaptation to a new culture when I moved to the United States. I used an "eco-map" to show Graciela the connections, or lack thereof, with her immediate world. We identified sources of support, such as the day care Azucena attended, one of the schools where Graciela worked, and an invitation to attend her coworker's church. I also started creating a genogram and gathered some family history as a way to gain a sense of history and an understanding of family patterns.

   Sessions 5-7. Graciela and Azucena came to therapy conjointly. Azucena was laughing with her mother when I went to meet them in the waiting room. They both had this glow that kind of let me know things were better now.

Therapist:	Tell me how things are going for you and Azucena. How have you been since I last saw you?
Graciela:	Well, we have been better. Azucena is enjoying her day care more and more. She adores her teacher, Elena, who seems to have a special place in her heart for Azucena. I have gotten to know Elena too, since she has invited both of us to a couple of parties. I feel like Elena understands what it is to be new in a foreign country, and I have not felt so alone. She is a good person to know.
Therapist:	It sounds like you have been reaching out to others. Wow!
Graciela:	Yes, I have not been crying as much, and Azucena seems to be happier and adjusting well to school. She is even potty trained now.
Therapist:	Lots of changes since I last saw you.
Azucena:	(She has been playing with the little kitchen. She moved towards her mother with a cup of tea inviting her to play.) Here! This is for you, "mamá." Tea for you.

   Most of Azucena's play focused on nurturance. She played with a doll, feeding her and changing her, and asked her mother to take part in her play. Azucena occasionally used the doll house to recreate scenes of what was going on at home with her mother. She also drew smiley faces on the chalkboard. I was a little bit surprised that she had the ability to draw such faces at such an early age. I commented on it and Graciela reinforced the idea that Azucena was artistically inclined, and had, in fact, been drawing those faces for a while. I wondered about the meaning of those smiley faces. Perhaps Azucena, in her own way, was trying to let her mother know that she was happy despite the adjustments.

   As Graciela was getting ready to leave, she told me she had met a man at one of the social gatherings at work. His name was Víctor and he was from Spain. She liked the way he played with Azucena at the party. Graciela also said that since she and Azucena were doing better, they might come back in a month instead of every other week. I agreed that they were doing better and that it was up to her to decide when to come back.

<u>Session 8.</u> A little over a month later, Graciela called to make an appointment. She sounded stressed over the phone. She came to the session without Azucena, who was at a party with some children from the day care.

Graciela:	I thought I was doing well. Azucena has been acting up lately, and I am starting to feel it is my fault again.
Therapist:	What do you mean? Has something happened since I saw you last?
Graciela:	Well, Víctor, the man I told you I had met at the social, and I have been going out. I really like him, and I think it is good for Azucena to have a male influence in her life. He is very good to her. But lately he has been coming over more and even spending some nights with us, and Azucena has really been acting up. It makes me think she is jealous that I am sharing some of my attention with him.
Therapist:	The last months have been quite intense for both of you, and in some ways all you have had is one another. Remember that any adjustment to a new situation is a process.
Graciela:	I guess you are right. I just want her to be happy, and I think Víctor would be really good for her.
Therapist:	It sounds like he brings many gifts into your life, for you and for Azucena. And gradually, she will adjust to him being in your lives if the relationship grows. But remember that this is an adult decision, and that in her head she may fear she is losing her mother if she has to share you with him. Give her time to adjust, continue to reinforce that you can love them both and that you are there for her. Let her know you love her. But it does sound like this situation has brought back some fears for you.
Graciela:	Well, Víctor and I had discussed the idea of him moving in with us. We would both save money that way. And if things go right, we may get married in the next six months. But I am feeling fearful again.
Therapist:	Wow! Those are big changes in your life. And I know how much you have been longing for a loving relationship with a man. Do you think he would be open to come to therapy with you for a couple of sessions? I wonder if that would help you both with this transition.

<u>Sessions 9-11.</u> About a month later, Graciela called to set up an appointment for a couples session. When I first met them, both partners smiled, and they had an aura of love around them. Víctor had moved in. They struggled at times with the new situation, and Graciela was worried that Víctor would leave. Víctor was not even aware that Graciela had been worried about him leaving. His concern was that the two of them were fighting more than usual. We worked on communication skills. We enacted a conflict scene in the session so they could both practice conflict resolution skills.

During those three conjoint sessions, we discussed different things related to their individual upbringings: family of origin influences, beliefs, personality traits, and similarities and differences about ways of being. While they both spoke Spanish, they were from different countries. They agreed that ultimately they both wanted to get married and become a family. I gave them a marital inventory that disclosed areas that could cause conflict. One of the areas was parenting. What role would Víctor play in parenting Azucena, and what differences did they have in their parenting styles? We agreed to include Azucena in a session.

Session 12. The couple and Azucena came to the session together. Graciela and Víctor had decided that they were going to get married and had already told Azucena.

Therapist:	You all look so good! How are you doing?
Graciela:	(while holding Azucena and looking at Víctor.) We are doing very good!
Therapist:	What about you, Víctor?
Víctor:	Really good! We have been great since last time we saw you a month ago.
Graciela:	We are doing so good that I even told Víctor today that I was wondering if we needed to continue to come. What do you think?
Therapist:	I always think you know best if you need to continue to come to therapy. And I tell my clients that even when you leave, you know the door is open to come back if the need arises. But I would agree that you have made great strides.

It was a time to celebrate their accomplishments and affirm them as individuals. I let them know that I was very proud of them and happy for them and that I felt honored to have been a part of their healing experience. My role was simply to encourage them, support them, and cheer with them as we reflected upon all they had achieved throughout the course of therapy.

Outcome

Graciela reported relief from her feelings of sadness within the first four weeks of treatment. She felt better adjusted to a new culture after the first six months following her move to the United States. Her feelings of isolation had decreased since she had developed new relationships. By the end of treatment, her depression had subsided completely. Azucena was rapidly becoming bilingual. The crying spells disappeared.

Mother and daughter were happy with Víctor in their lives. In fact, they were full of joy! Not only did Graciela grow as an individual, she also grew as a mother and a woman. Azucena grew along with her, and their bond strengthened. In some ways, being in a new culture allowed them to become closer emotionally than they had been before in Chile, where Graciela's parents had taken a co-parenting role with Azucena.

Discussion

At a time in which Graciela was feeling isolated from the world of her culture, family, and country, it was crucial that she had a place where she would feel emotionally supported, connected, cared for, and understood. I believe the context of therapy provided that for her. I really want to make the point that reactions to the process of adjusting to new cultures, values, and ways of being can be easily mistaken for dysfunction. I also think that when working with clients whose first language is not English, it is important to assess their ability to converse in the second language and to determine if they can feel and express emotions in it. As a non-American, I can relate to the experience of having to adjust to a new culture. Although English has been my most frequently used language for the last decade, I still struggle for words to express the intensity of a wide variety of emotions. If I were a client, the ability of a therapist to communicate with me in my first language would greatly facilitate expression and enhance the therapeutic process. A common feeling immigrants share is the sense of not belonging in either culture. In fact, very often, immigrants feel as if they are living between worlds, not fully belonging to the new culture and separated from their own. As a therapist, I believe that children and adults are very resilient. Although single parents have many challenges in raising their children, they also have the potential to raise healthy and well-adjusted children. In fact, I always marvel at how people cope, make it through hardships, and later blossom. Just a miracle!

References

Casado, M., Young, M.E., & Rasmus, S.D. (2002). *Exercises in Family Therapy.* Upper Saddle River, New Jersey: Merrill/Prentice Hall.

Landreth, G. (1991). *Play Therapy: The Art of the Relationship.* Levittown, Pennsylvania: Accelerated Development.

Satir, V. (1976). *Making Contact.* Berkley, California: Celestial Arts.

Biographical Statement

Montserrat Casado, Ph.D., is an assistant professor in Counselor Education and coordinator of the Play Therapy Certificate program in the Department of Child, Family and Community Sciences at the University of Central Florida, Orlando. She is a licensed marriage and family therapist and a registered play therapist. Montse coauthored *Exercises in Family Therapy* (Prentice Hall, 2002) and *Instructor's Manual to Family Therapy: History, Theory, and Practice,* 2nd ed. (Prentice Hall, 2002). She has also co-authored several articles about family therapy, including "Promoting strengths and celebrating culture: Working with Hispanic families" (*The Family Journal*, 1998); and "A family affair: Helping children and families deal with trauma" (*Association for Play Therapy, Inc. Newsletter*, 2001). You can reach Montse at mcasado@mail.ucf.edu.

Rename the Blame Frame

Collie W. Conoley

Collie Conoley leads a university team in a successful attempt to expand the focus from a depressed individual to the family system. Conoley takes honest pleasure in theorizing with his graduate students. He opens everything up for discussion with the idea that multiple perspectives create multiple solutions and the risk that freewheeling hypotheses can create a family that exists only in the therapy team's collective imagination.

R

andy's mother, Ellen, called the university training facility to schedule an appointment with our family intervention team. I'm a professor and supervisor and the leader of a therapy team consisting of seven graduate students in marriage and family counseling.

Ellen was worried about 14-year-old Randy, whom she described as avoiding school and being uncooperative at home. The intake worker told Ellen that a team of therapists would see her for a four-session intervention. Ellen agreed to an initial session to include her husband, Ed, 42; and three sons, Ray, 18; Randy, 14; and Wayne, 10. In accord with our sliding-scale fee schedule, this family would pay $5 per session.

■ Conceptualization

Theory excites me! Our training group is committed to the Milan Systemic approach that uses three primary principles: (1) hypothesizing; (2) circularity; and (3) neutrality. *Hypothesizing* is a systematic process of guessing what is going on. *Circularity* is a process of feeding back to the family what is heard from them, usually in the form of questions. It is a process of ensuring that each member's perspective or point of view is heard by everyone, including the therapeutic team. *Neutrality* refers to the attitude of the therapist as expressed by perpetual curiosity about what everyone has to say and taking everyone's side. Reframing is used only when everyone is portrayed positively.

The team met to discuss the family before the initial session. Of course, we expect to update our conceptualization after each meeting, but by way of getting our systemic juices flowing, we take part in a speculative team discussion in order to hypothesize about the family even before the first session.

Hypothesizing is based on the typical individual and family developmental influences. What could 14-year-old Randy, the center of his mother's initial concern, be up to? Developmentally, we expect that he will be more attentive to peers than his parents and may be getting involved with girls. We hypothesized that something could be frustrating about his peer relationships. Also, Randy is a middle child and may feel ignored, believing that his siblings receive most of the family's attention. Perhaps Randy is doing poorly in school, and the family is unable to help.

More speculation. The older boy could be graduating from high school this year and heading off to college, thereby producing stress and tension. Is this family doing a good job of preparing children to be independent? Perhaps the parents are having difficulty with intimacy or aggravation on the job. Maybe the grandparents are in failing health and need more of the parents' attention.

Whew! That was a wild ride on the road of possible family bumps and detours. By encouraging such divergent hypothesizing, I'm trying to get the therapy team to open its ears. Multiple perspectives create multiple solutions. The downside or danger is that our hypotheses could create a family that exists only in our team's imagination.

---■ **Process**

Session 1. Ellen and her three boys arrived without the dad. I expressed delight to meet the family members and regret that the father was not present. They completed the brief biographical forms and were informed of the limits of confidentiality. I told the family about our therapy team approach and the advantage it offered: many heads are better than one. They agreed to the use of a therapy team and videotaping for supervision and research purposes. The therapy team was introduced as a group and then left for the observation room.

The family had moved to the country, 3 miles outside a small rural town, to have a peaceful, safe place to live. The younger boy, Wayne, was the biological son of Ellen and Ed. The older two boys, Randy and Ray, were Ellen's biological sons but not Ed's, and they had no relationship with their biological father. Ed and Ellen were high school graduates but had not attended college. Both held blue-collar jobs that paid slightly above minimum wage.

I do not start with the person who is the most upset or the person who was described as problematic. I want to avoid the blaming that is associated with the "identified patient." In this case, I began with the youngest child.

Therapist:	You are the youngest, Wayne? How old are you?
Wayne:	I'm 10, almost 11. I'm in the fourth grade.
Therapist:	And what do you like most about fourth grade?
Wayne:	I have a really nice teacher this year. She lets us play games in class.
Therapist:	Sounds like fun. What is your favorite thing to do at home?
Wayne:	I like playing with Randy. When he lets me.
Therapist:	That brings me around to Randy. So Wayne enjoys playing with you, but the feeling isn't mutual?
Randy:	You could say that.
Wayne:	Randy tells me to go away (begins crying).
Therapist:	Randy, you are important to Wayne.

I positively framed "important to" instead of the negative "disappointing to."

Randy:	Yeah. I just don't feel like playing with him anymore.
Therapist:	What has changed?
Randy:	I don't know.
Therapist:	A mystery! Does anyone have a clue?

I used a tentative tone in asking for help in the investigation into the causes of Randy's feelings. To ask for guesses is to acknowledge that no one but Randy could presume to be certain of his feelings. Introducing hypothesizing through curiosity, tentativeness, inclusivity, and a positive frame about issues is central to our approach. We hope the family will eventually pick up these techniques and use them.

Ellen:	This is why I brought us here. Randy doesn't want to do anything anymore with anyone.
Therapist:	So you are concerned about Randy, how he has changed.

The word *concerned* is chosen even though there was irritation or mild anger in the mother's voice. I go for the positive frame.

Ellen:	He used to enjoy school, and he paid attention to Wayne.
Therapist:	And you're worried about these changes. Randy, what do you enjoy doing these days?
Randy:	Nothing. I just don't feel like doing anything anymore. (He starts to cry.)
Therapist:	Ellen, what do you think this means that Randy is crying and telling us that he cannot think of anything that he enjoys doing?
Ellen:	Well, it worries me a lot. This is why I wanted to come see you.

The team was surprised by the problem, because it didn't match the telephone intake problem statement. However, often parents do not have the traditional psychological diagnostic vocabulary at their disposal.

Therapist:	You have seen Randy crying, and he's withdrawing from his normal activities?
Ellen:	Yes, and it's gotten steadily worse for the last month. Maybe since school started.
Therapist:	Is that how you see it Randy?
Randy:	I don't know.

Ray, the older brother, communicated his embarrassment at Randy's crying by obvious disgust and irritation. I asked how Ed (father and husband) would react if he were present. The family agreed that Ed's reaction to Randy would be the same as Ray's.

I announced a break to consult with the therapy team. It's usually beneficial for the family to observe a consultation between therapist and team, but since this was a new team, I decided against it. A new team tends to avoid speaking out for fear of harming the family or making a negative impression on peers and supervisor.

During our private discussion, the team focused on Randy's depression exclusively. They observed that Randy did not change his affect throughout the session. The team recommended that I talk with Randy alone to explore suicide potential.

Randy's one-on-one interview revealed high suicide risk. I did not feel assured that he would not make an attempt. He became even more listless and depressed as I asked about his experience. I was convinced that there was a real danger and recommended hospitalization.

<u>Session 2.</u> Two weeks later and just two days after Randy's discharge from the hospital, we saw the family again. I had talked with Ed and tried to persuade him to attend. I told him how important, how potentially helpful, his viewpoint was to me. I wanted to counter the predictable feelings of guilt and shame that are often associated with having a suicidal child. The father attended.

We reviewed the confidentiality and structure of the sessions for Ed's benefit. Ed was reserved and defensive.

I asked the family what they thought of the hospital. There was a hush except for Randy. He talked easily about his hospital experience. I asked what the hospital staff thought the problem was and if anything had changed since Randy had come home. Ed angrily stated that the hospital blamed him for everything. I was astonished or, at least, acted as if I were.

Therapist: How did they think it was your fault?

Ed told me to ask Randy.

Randy: The therapists said that I am depressed because I'm holding in my anger. I'm supposed to express my anger toward Dad directly, or I'll get depressed again.

Other family members confirmed Randy's impression, having heard this account at family counseling sessions. Ed and Ray were unhappy with the "express your anger at Dad" notion, while Ellen and Wayne (the youngest son) approved. Ed said he only went to one of the family sessions because Randy was encouraged to express anger at him.

I figured it was time to meet with my team.

The team observed that the hospital's "express your anger at Dad" intervention seemed to work for Randy and perhaps for Ellen and Wayne. However, Ed and Ray rejected it. This split in the family's response to the "answer" was, in itself, a problem. Answers that are perceived to blame make a bad situation worse.

The team hypothesized that the family members were at different places on a continuum of needing closeness and wanting distance. Ed and Ray leaned toward distance, with Wayne and Ellen in the closeness camp. Randy was in between. With this perspective, no one gets blamed. The team advised me to listen for opportunities to reduce blaming or shaming and to enhance mutual support for solutions. Ultimately, it's the family that decides on the utility of our brilliant hypothesis.

Back in the family session, I asked Randy what he hoped would change in the family if he expressed his anger directly. What good would the anger do? Randy started crying. He said that he wanted his Dad to spend more time with him like he used to do. I took this opportunity of a suggested solution to move away from a blaming conceptualization.

Therapist: So you're looking for a way to invite your Dad to do more activities with you?

That conceptualization fit for Randy, Ellen, and Wayne. However, Ed and Ray seemed confused. They had no idea that Randy was asking for greater intimacy with his father. The family recounted that when they lived in the city they had shared good times together, and Ed took the lead in organizing family activities. I kept the conversations focused on how each person enjoyed the fun and how they would like to rekindle the warmth. Ed had been the major force in the family's move out to the country, and now he was seen to have "abandoned" the family. I could see how he would feel blamed and defensive.

Ray, the eldest, wasn't put out with the family's move. Ray just wanted to spend time with his friends and was looking forward to going into the armed forces. He had little interest in getting closer to the rest of the family. Given his age, Ray's leaving home was appropriate. However, Ray believed his brother, Randy, should think and feel the same way.

Sessions 3 and 4. Themes for these last two sessions were planning enjoyable family activities (mostly without Ray), asking for closeness and responding when asked, making friends, and planning for the future. The team was worried that Ray could become the focus of blame because he was the only person wanting to sepa-rate. Therefore, I tried to normalize and help differentiate Ray's desires as being typi-cal of an individual old enough to leave home. At the same time, I wanted Ray to accept that his stage of development was different from Randy's. I devoted time to ex-plore what holidays would be like without Ray and what life would be like for Ed and Ellen when all of the kids left home.

◾ Outcome

In the process of addressing the presenting problem of Randy's depression, our team helped everyone in the family. Ellen wanted more intimacy with Ed and got it. Ray's leaving home was facilitated. Ray was encouraged to believe that leaving home was good for him *and* not harmful to his family. Both Randy and Wayne got a lot of sup-port in counseling, and Randy's depression lifted. We made sure nobody became the designated scapegoat.

◾ Discussion

This family raised provocative issues for the team and me. What would have hap-pened in the first session if Ed had showed up? Would hospitalization for suicide risk have been avoided? Were we right to recommend hospitalization? Another issue was the definition of the problem. Depression is often conceptualized as anger turned in-ward, so the hospital staff's idea of turning Randy's anger outward seemed to make sense.

Problems can be looked at from different angles. As I've said, directing Randy's anger at his absent Dad seemed to make sense, but when a solution creates more problems than it solves, it must be reexamined. As an alternative to the anger-turned-inward concept, our team defined depression as being a result of not experiencing closeness in the family. This conceptualization was useful for this family, and the asso-ciated solutions fell right into place.

Biographical Statement

Collie W. Conoley is a professor in the counseling psychology program at Texas A&M University. He has worked in private practice, at an adolescent inpatient hospital, in a university counseling center, and in community mental health centers. You can reach Collie at collie-conoley@tamu.edu.

5

An Affair to Forget

Phyllis Erdman

David, a substance abusing teenager, and his family were referred by his probation officer. Erdman decided that the marriage was the "sick patient;" the disease was an extramarital affair.

Erdman demonstrates the use of the Global Assessment of Relational Functioning, a scale in the DSM-IV. She uses a reflecting team as a training strategy and relies on emotionally focused therapy as a therapeutic modality.

What I value especially is Erdman's struggle with an unpleasant outcome. Things just didn't turn out very well. Erdman says, "Bowen indicates the importance of knowing when an emotional system is dead and in need of a decent burial. I think I have become more aware of that and am more willing to surrender my responsibility for creating life."

Rick, 48, and Paula, 46, came to family therapy because their son, David, 17, had been involved in a drug possession incident, and family therapy was required as part of his probation. The first few sessions included David, both parents, and their daughter, Jessica, 12. Rick didn't want counseling to focus only on David's drug problem. He saw more significant problems, especially David's oppositional attitude and increasing hostility. Rick and David had frequent arguments about David staying out too late and drinking with his friends. Rick believed that Paula and David were aligned against him.

David's probation officer was familiar with our services as a training facility and referred the family. She warned they would probably be resistant. As the director of the university clinic, I decided to work with the family myself and allow students to observe. My initial intent was to see the family for a few sessions and then gradually transition the case to a student. I changed my mind and kept them for the entire course of treatment because I felt challenged by their "stuckness" and saw a chance to illustrate an emotionally focused approach for my students.

Conceptualization

My initial assessment of the family was based on the Global Assessment of Relational Functioning (GARF), a scale in the *DSM-IV* (American Psychological Association, 1994) that measures families on three factors:

1. *Problem solving skills.* Describes the ability to negotiate rules and goals, communicate, and resolve conflict.
2. *Organizational skills.* Describes the usefulness of roles and boundaries, hierarchical functioning, coalitions, and distribution of power and control.
3. *Emotional climate.* Describes the quality of caring and empathy, degree of attachment and commitment, mutual affective responsiveness, and quality of sexual functioning.

Scores on the GARF range from 1 to 100, with the highest score representing the highest degree of functioning. After the first three interviews, my graduate students and I concurred that this family rated in the mid- to high 40s on all three scales of the GARF, which indicates unsatisfactory functioning.

The family's *problem solving skills* were hampered by their inability to adapt to family and individual transitions. An example was the couple's unwillingness to look honestly at their marital problems. As both children were approaching or already in adolescence, the typical problems associated with this stage of family development (e.g., children's struggles with independence) piled stress onto an already tense relationship. Family members were sucked into behavioral problems to such a depth that they were unable to move to the next developmental stage.

Organizational skills were hindered by the intergenerational alliances between Paula and David and the lack of a clear spousal/parental subsystem. Many of the decisions, especially those surrounding parental authority, were made on the basis of dominance and control, which resulted in a rigid and unbalanced distribution of power within the family. Paula perceived Rick as having too much control over everyone in the family.

The *emotional climate* was bitter and detached, as Rick and Paula maintained protective shields against their own vulnerabilities. The couple's lack of trust in each other was manifested in an unsatisfactory sexual relationship.

Based on this miserable GARF assessment, I decided to address the emotional rigidity, as well as the interactional process, through an emotionally focused approach. In emotionally focused therapy (EFT), there is a constant shift between the intrapsychic experience and the interpersonal context. This approach would allow me to restructure the system into more appropriate subsystems (e.g., parental and spousal), thereby addressing the interactional and organizational problems within the family. I could also address the emotional climate by helping Rick and Paula express and validate their vulnerabilities and insecurities of emotional attachment.

Emotionally focused therapy is grounded in an attachment theory framework, and the goal is to change both the couple's interactional cycle and each spouse's experience of the relationship. The focus is on identifying the repetitive interactional sequences of behavior (e.g., Rick's pursuing Paula and Paula's withdrawing) and reframing the problem in terms of underlying feelings of attachment.

Attachment theory deals with a person's perceived secure relationship with his or her primary caregiver during infancy (Bowlby, 1988). The nature of this attachment and the role of emotion in defining intimate relationships are crucial concepts of EFT (Johnson & Greenberg, 1995). Disowning primary feelings (e.g., Paula and Rick's hurt, insecurity, rejection, and fear) results in ineffective communication between them (e.g., blaming, accusing, and withdrawing from each other).

Rick: I'm just trying to protect my children and set rules for their going out and such. But she (Paula) undoes everything I try to do.
Paula: I just think sometimes that Rick doesn't understand what it's like to be a teenager and need a little freedom.
Therapist: So, Rick, you don't think that you and Paula are pulling together.
Rick: (throwing his hands up in despair) There's no way I'm going to get between David and Paula.

Clearly, parent alliances with the children provoked marital conflict. After a few sessions, David had received permission from his probation officer to transfer to a male counselor, whom he felt would relate to him better. Rick, Paula, and Jessica continued to see me with a goal of improving communication. Rick's first priority for counseling was to "forgive and forget," and Paula's first priority was to "learn how to deal with pain." When I asked for more information about priorities, they both indicated they preferred not to talk about it with Jessica present and smiled at each other knowingly. I scheduled some later sessions with only Rick and Paula. We were down to the essential twosome.

There was another piece of data that influenced my thinking about this case.

Paula:	(smiling and looking down) You tell her.
Rick:	(smiling sarcastically) Well, it's your thing. You did it.
Therapist:	(after a long silence) What is it that you want me to know?
Rick:	(no longer smiling) I can't even say the word. (long pause) It was her seeing somebody else. Let's just call it "the thing."
Therapist:	So, Paula, you had an affair?
Rick:	(nervous laughing) Not just one, three.

The marriage was the sick patient here! Any attempt to divert my efforts to the children would waste precious time. Because of the mistrust that surrounded Paula's affairs, I decided to bring them to the forefront. I used Glass and Wright's (1990) approach to diffuse the secrecy of the affairs and to enhance marital intimacy. Their approach is based on a metaphorical perception of infidelity referred to as "moving walls and windows." The idea is to discuss the affair in an attempt to shift the walls and windows in the extramarital triangle so that the spouse is "inside" with walls around the marriage and the affair is "outside" with windows into it.

This couple's struggle to not allow themselves to become vulnerable with each other was so deeply embedded in intergenerational attachment issues and so strongly reinforced by the multiple affairs that neither could make the first move toward change. During the sessions Rick lashed out with sarcasm and blame, and Paula sheepishly smiled and responded to both Rick and me with, "I don't know." My interventions brought me "Yes, buts" from both partners.

I used a reflecting team (Anderson, 1987) to bring new information into the therapy room. The reflecting team usually consisted of five doctoral-level counseling interns who viewed the sessions through a one-way mirror. Midway into the session, I reversed the mirror by switching the lights off in the counseling room and on in the observation room. Then my clients and I would observe the team members talking about the session. The team's tone is positive and tentative. The clients are regarded as the true experts on their lives and are free to accept or reject the team's perspective.

Process

Sessions 1-4. All four family members (Rick, Paula, David, and Jessica) attended the first three sessions. After David received his probation officer's permission to transfer to another counselor, we were down to three. The focus was on family issues.

Sessions 5-11. Rebuilding trust and possibilities for forgiveness were at the top of my agenda. I used a genogram to gather background data. Rick's first marriage was ended by his wife for no reason he could identify. Paula described her former spouse as a selfish, unfaithful alcoholic who divorced her for another woman. I thought it would be important to explore what Paula's affairs meant to each one, as both Paula and Rick had been abandoned in previous relationships.

By the ninth session Paula indicated that the stress was extremely high and she wasn't sure she could continue with therapy. She complained that sex was a major problem.

Paula:	Rick acts like he doesn't want to get near me. If we have sex, I initiate it, and I don't know if he even likes it. It's like he's not there.
Rick:	Everything has to meet her needs. That's all she thinks about and always has.
Paula:	If you would just forget about what happened, we could go on.
Therapist:	You'd really like Rick to forgive you for the affairs, wouldn't you, Paula?
Rick:	That sounds easy, but I can't.
Therapist:	(to Rick) No, it doesn't sound easy. What do you think needs to happen? What do you need from Paula to help you let go of some of it?
Rick:	I don't think there's anything that Paula can do now. It's been done.

When the intensity got this extreme, the couple would somehow redirect to a child-focused problem. During the 11th session, I requested the input of the reflecting team. The team told Rick and Paula that they were stuck and neither was ready to change. They commented on Rick's difficulty in trying to forgive Paula and their sense of hopelessness about the relationship if forgiveness couldn't occur. The team reframed this as an opportunity for Rick and Paula to open up and discuss old issues in order to rebuild their relationship on solid ground. We contracted for five more sessions to continue processing the affairs. Rick and Paula gave me permission to prevent them from distracting themselves from facing the meaning of the affairs.

Sessions 12-14. Jessica showed up at the 12th session, which was devoted to Jessica's refusal to complete her homework and how Rick's insistence on her doing so made him look like the "bad guy" in the family. During the next two sessions, we dealt exclusively with Jessica's homework problems.

Sessions 15-28. Rick and Paula resumed marital therapy but continued to avoid discussing the extramarital affairs. I became frustrated with them and invited a male colleague in as a co-therapist. We asked Rick and Paula to bring a list of questions they wanted to ask each other as well as things they wanted to tell the other. Paula, as usual, did not complete her assignment. Rick, as usual, came with a long list of questions about the affairs. Paula continued to respond with vague, non-committal replies.

Rick:	I just want to know what they gave you that I didn't.
Paula:	I don't know.
Rick:	(agitated voice) Well, you're bound to know why you slept with them. Was it just sex or what, Paula?
Paula:	He keeps throwing it up at me. If I tell him what happened, he'll use it against me.
Therapist:	I'm wondering what each of you needs from the other to be able to be vulnerable.
Rick:	I won't do that again. I was vulnerable. I trusted her completely. Never again.

On another occasion, Rick expressed his ambivalence.

Rick: Sometimes when I push you away, I want to be hugged.

The double messages he sent Paula confused her so much, though, that she didn't know whether to reach out or not. In response to her own fears of being rejected, she chose not to take the risk, leaving both alone.

Session 29. Rick informed me that his father had died the previous week. Rick was responsible for all of the funeral arrangements, although he and his father had a very distant relationship. This was a significant session, because I learned how Rick had learned to protect his emotions in his original family. Now he was still protecting himself by refusing to reach out and ask Paula for emotional support during the stressful time of his father's death. It was also clear how Paula, afraid of Rick's refusing her offer of support, maintained the distance.

Rick:	The burden always falls on me. I guess I'm the only one in my family who can handle it.
Therapist:	What are your feelings toward your father now that he's dead?
Rick:	I feel like I should be sad, but I'm not. What hurts is that no one in my family thought about me and my feelings. They just assumed I would take care of everything. There it goes again. I'm being put upon.
Therapist:	You feel sort of betrayed by them. Again.
Rick:	Yeah, but I'm used to it. (laughing) I got my walls and I can hide behind them.
Therapist:	And if you removed your walls?
Rick:	Nope, I've been hurt too many times.
Therapist:	How did Paula help you through this, the funeral and all?
Rick:	I didn't need her to. I handled it.
Therapist:	Paula, what did you think Rick needed from you?
Paula:	I don't know. He'd never tell me.

It was apparent that neither trusted the other, and I began to consider individual sessions. Both acknowledged that they avoid closeness and wait for the other to do something different. Rick also expressed fear that he is pushing his son, David, away, just as his father pushed him away. I raised the possibility of individual sessions, and Rick eagerly agreed to it but emphasized that Paula needed help more than he did.

Sessions 30-35. I had six individual sessions with Paula, during which we discussed family-of-origin issues. Paula and her mother were emotionally detached. Her mother dominated Paula. Paula resented this but didn't know how to break away. Now she felt pulled between her mother and Rick, with both trying to control her. Paula was guarded with me.

Therapist:	It sounds as if you resent your mother's intrusion, especially when it causes conflict between you and Rick.
Paula:	(cautiously) I guess sometimes I'd like her to leave me, us, alone. But she means well. And Rick can't understand that.

Therapist: It's difficult being pulled between your mother and your husband.

I pushed hard to help Paula see the impact her mother had on her marital relationship. I sensed her reluctance. She suggested that it was time for Rick to rejoin her in the sessions. The reflecting team made a comment that definitely got Paula's attention.

Reflecting Team: We appreciate how hard it was for Paula to come to counseling this week. No one ever stood up to Mom, and if they did they were severely punished. Understandably, Paula finds it difficult to stand up to Rick and tell him what she really wants. Just as she couldn't with Mom. We wonder if she's afraid of being abandoned by Rick just as she was by her mother.

Paula continued two more sessions of individual therapy. She was in conflict over hating what her mother did to her (abandonment) and feeling as if she, nevertheless, owed love to her mother.

Therapist: What was it like for you when Mom wasn't there for you emotionally or even physically?
Paula: (beginning to get teary eyed) Alone . . . scared.

Sessions 36–38. These conjoint sessions were hot with anger and projection. I intended to share some of the information Paula had given me, as she and I had agreed, so that Rick might have a better understanding of her pain. But the arguing and blaming was so intense, all I could do was try to hang in there and defuse the negative emotionality.

Rick: We're back at square one. Things are getting out of hand with David again.
Paula: That's because you won't let him tell you what's going on. You want to control him so much, you're pushing him away. (Paula cries and attempts to leave the room.)
Therapist: Paula, come back. I know both of you are hurting a lot now.
Paula: (interrupts) He doesn't have any idea what I'm going through. (sobbing)
Therapist: What is it like hearing that from Paula?

Rick shrugged his shoulders and wouldn't respond.

Sessions 39–42. To allow Rick the same opportunity as Paula, I offered him four individual sessions. During the first session, we discussed their current stalemate.

Rick: I'm waiting for Paula to prove herself, and I do this by ignoring her.
Therapist: You mean to prove her love after the affairs?
Rick: Yeah, I know she's hurting, but so am I.
Therapist: And what keeps you from telling her this?
Rick: Emotions mean weakness, and that means being vulnerable, and then someone can seize upon you.

Therapist:	So much energy is going into protecting yourself.
Rick:	I'm really terribly lonely and scared to death of losing her and the kids.
Therapist:	Keeping your family at a safe distance guarantees that you'll lose them.

Rick discussed the pain of his relationship with his father and his own loneliness and fears. I asked him why he could be so open with me. He said that I was safe.

The Final Session. They were seriously contemplating divorce. Paula couched it in terms of needing "time out" for a while, and Rick presented it as an inevitable response to their impasse. They verbally attacked each other and seemed more distant than ever.

As a result of my frustration with the lack of positive movement, I confronted them strongly with questions about what they were both wanting now to help them clarify to each other their commitment to the relationship.

The next four sessions were either canceled by them or by me due to other commitments. I was unhappy with how things were going, and now I suspect that I was subconsciously avoiding further contacts. About five weeks after the last conjoint session, Rick called to tell me that they were separating. I offered individual sessions to both, but they declined.

◼ Outcome

Three months later Rick called to inform me that they were divorced. I offered additional sessions to both of them, either individual sessions or conjoint to resolve divorce issues. Neither wanted to continue, so I closed the case. I contacted Rick and Paula two years later to conduct a follow-up interview, and they both indicated that they would prefer individual interviews. This is by no means a typical request I make of my clients, but in spite of the outcome of the therapy, I felt a closeness to both Rick and Paula as well as curiosity. I wanted to know how they were dealing with the divorce, and I wanted feedback on the counseling process.

The most important thing I learned from the interviews was that Rick had known all along that he was not capable of forgiving Paula for the affairs.

Rick:	Really, I scrapped the marriage a long time ago and was coming to counseling more for myself.
Therapist:	I didn't know that. I thought you were really working on getting back together.
Rick:	Don't get me wrong. I wasn't stringing you along in the counseling, but I knew I had to work on myself. It was me who couldn't make it work. I wouldn't let it work.

Paula shared similar perceptions of what had occurred in counseling.

| Paula: | Rick could talk a lot about what needed to be done, but he couldn't do it. I don't know why. He was more invested in coming to counseling, but I was more invested in actually doing something. |

Therapist: Was there anything I could have done differently to help either of
                you move forward?
Paula: No. You would have had to turn the clock back 10 years. I don't think
                he'll ever forgive me, and that's OK. I'll take the blame.

I think that Rick used counseling primarily as a way to end the relationship on
friendly terms. Who needs enemies? He also wanted personal growth from it, which I
believe he received.

Both Rick and Paula indicated that the counseling occurred too late in the relationship, 10 years after the first affair, and that had they come sooner, they might have
saved the marriage.

Rick was still hurting a lot and actually felt more insecure now than right after
the divorce. He still maintained an emotional distance from Paula, even though they
saw each other periodically, and indicated he "had worked too hard to keep her away
to allow her to get close now" and that he had "put the walls up and double-bolted
the door." For her part, Paula came to realize how much she had depended on Rick.

Therapist: What has the most difficult thing been for you after the divorce?
Paula: Being alone. Having no one to depend on and no one for support. I
                have to make my own decisions and use my own judgment. I hadn't
                realized how much I had depended on Rick.

Although Paula was more reserved in the therapy sessions and, on the surface,
appeared to be getting less from therapy than Rick, I think she may have actually
made more internal changes. She indicated that she had a better relationship with her
mother and that "the door that used to be closed was now cracked."

■ Discussion

I used emotionally focused therapy with Rick and Paula, considering their GARF assessment. This approach provides a way of conceptualizing and intervening at both
the intrapsychic and the interactional level and addresses the GARF's emotional, organizational, and problem solving components. I hoped that EFT would be a catalyst.

The caveat that I failed to heed was that both Rick and Paula preferred the risk
of divorce to the risk inherent in changing. Although I initially viewed their high level
of tolerance for their relationship as a strength that would keep them together, I later
viewed it as an obstacle that prevented them both from making the first move. They
were locked in a downward spiral.

Success with EFT requires each partner's acceptance and validation of the
other's phenomenological world, but this can only occur in the context of a safe environment. Rick started counseling with an attitude that it wouldn't work, and he
relentlessly refused to acknowledge Paula's point of view. No safety there! Paula, on
the other hand, could never reassure Rick that it was emotionally safe for him to validate her, because when he did try, she viewed it as a way to usurp more power in
the relationship rather than to balance the power. And then there was the awful damage wrought by her affairs. In the follow-up interview, Rick told me that he could have
started the ball rolling by forgiving, but he just couldn't do it.

Perhaps if I had exposed their mutual disinclination to risk change earlier, I could have prevented the long duration of 43 sessions. With the benefit of hindsight, I would have started individual sessions earlier and I would have found a more effective way to introduce the individual issues back into the relationship. Rick developed a closer alliance with me than with Paula, and he was able to express his vulnerabilities to me, but not to her, out of fear of Paula's rejection. I would probably spend less time processing the specifics of the affairs and emphasize more strongly the concept of forgiving and its role in Rick's life.

Bowen indicates the importance of knowing when an emotional system is dead and in need of a decent burial. I think I have become more aware of that and am more willing to surrender my responsibility for creating life.

References

Andersen, T. (1987). The reflecting team: Dialogue and meta-dialogue in clinical work *Family Process, 26*, 415–428.

American Psychiatric Association. (1994). *Diagnostic and Statistical Manual of Mental Disorders* (4th ed.). Washington, D.C. Author.

Bowlby, J. (1988). *A Secure Base: Parent–child Attachment and Healthy Human Development*. New York: Basic Books.

Glass, S. P., & Wright, T. I., (1990). *Reconstructing After Extramarital Involvement*. Workshop presented at the AAMFT National Conference (AAMFT Learning Edge Series Video).

Johnson, S. M., & Greenberg, L. S. (1995). The emotionally focused approach to problems in adult attachment. In N. S. Jacobson & A. S. Gurman (Eds.), *Clinical Handbook of Couple Therapy*. New York: Guilford.

Biographical Statement

Phyllis Erdman, Ph.D., is professor and head of the Department of Counseling at Texas A&M University-Commerce and teaches marriage and family counseling courses. She is a licensed professional counselor, a licensed marriage and family therapist, and a clinical member and approved supervisor with the American Association for Marriage and Family Therapy. Phyllis's publications include "Let the Genogram Speak: Curiosity, Circularity, and Creativity in Family History" (*Journal of Family Psychotherapy*, 1995) and "Conceptualizing Parent Adolescent Conflict: Applications from Systems and Attachment Theories" (*The Family Journal of Psychotherapy*, 2000). You can reach her at phyllis_erdman@tamu-commerce.edu.

6

Losses and Gains

Marcheta Evans

The client, a 50-year-old woman, was referred by her pastor following the death of her twin daughter. Subsequently, Evans brought the surviving family members into counseling and helped them grieve.

Beginning private practitioners may identify with Evans's discomfort with collecting fees from an emotionally distraught person. Evans is also forthcoming about her own struggle with loss and subsequent spiritual confusion. Evans acknowledges a force at work that transcends therapeutic strategies: Time heals all wounds.

When I took on this case, I was an assistant professor of counselor education, and I saw clients for 20 hours a week at a private office I shared with a colleague. I had a contract with the Alabama Department of Human Resources. The cases assigned to me were usually nonvoluntary and court appointed.

Betty, 50 years old and African-American, was one of the first cases I worked with that was not appointed by the state. She was referred by her pastor following the death of her 10-year-old twin daughter, Brooke, from heart failure during a routine tonsillectomy. Michael was the surviving fraternal twin.

Betty's pastor referred her to me because she requested an African-American woman. She had had a negative experience working with a Caucasian male therapist. Betty had also seen a psychiatrist right after Brooke died but did not feel comfortable with him, either. She reported he really could not communicate with her. The psychiatrist had prescribed Prozac, an antidepressant, but she complained that it didn't help and, therefore, she had stopped taking it.

Betty arrived in my office extremely depressed. She was also worried that seeing a counselor would appear on her insurance record, so she opted to pay in cash. Later, I found out that there was more to this.

I asked about including her husband, Fred, in the interviews. She said that she needed to get her own act together first but was open to bringing in Fred later on.

Conceptualization

Betty had been employed as a clinical social worker, so she entered into the counseling process with a working knowledge of theory and some ideas about how she wanted counseling to go. She told me that a rational, action-oriented approach was what she wanted and needed.

Betty's presenting problem was depression; secondary issues were difficulty in dealing with loss, anger, spiritual confusion, and marital conflict. After encouraging the expression of all the emotions, thoughts, beliefs, and issues about the tragic loss and her relationships with significant individuals, we jointly developed therapeutic structure and goal-setting. Primary areas of concern were 1) the loss of her daughter; 2) her relationship with her son; 3) her relationship with her husband; 4) her relationships with her siblings and mother, which incorporated cultural issues; 5) her relationship with God and spirituality. I saw a need to focus on Betty's level of emotional detachment. She knew in her head that she needed help but demonstrated flat affect and a strong need for control. I felt there were also issues of guilt. Also, at the onset, I wanted to deal with confidentiality concerns due to her husband's prominent local image. What's more, I worried that my relatively young age would get in the way of her trusting that I could understand her.

Therapy proceeded from an Adlerian perspective and eventually incorporated Dinkmeyer's views on family therapy. The counseling process focused on the family constellation, mutual respect, encouragement, taking responsibility for one's behaviors, and an added affective component that dealt with the stages of grief. There was a cultural factor in my counseling because Betty, like me, is an African-American woman. At the start I saw Betty as an individual client, but later I brought her family into the sessions.

▦ Process

Individual Counseling with Betty, 24 Sessions. At the initial visit, I talked about who I am, my education, credentials, counseling philosophy, issues of confidentiality, and fees. Pretty standard. Then, of course, I started asking questions. I learned that Betty had been a social worker and was familiar with counseling. She had been working at home since the birth of the twins. Near the end of the session, Betty expressed concern about my age.

Betty: I don't mean to offend you, but I think you may be too young to help me. You just haven't lived long enough to experience this type of hurt.

Therapist: First of all, Betty, I'm older than I look. Is 37 old enough? But I also want you to know that I have experienced losses. Earlier this year, I lost my best friend to AIDS. Within the past year, my father-in-law was killed by a stroke, and my sister-in-law died from a brain tumor. I also know that these losses are not equivalent to losing a child.

This disclosure eased her mind. At the end of the session. I asked her to think about whether she wanted to return. The decision was hers. Two days later, Betty called to set up her next appointment, and counseling began in earnest.

Therapist: Betty, tell me more about what your life has become since Brooke died.

Betty: Over the last several months, I have basically become a hermit. I rarely leave the house, except to take my son to school. I do not really care about how I look. I haven't been to get my hair fixed in a very long time. I am just so tired. We have a housekeeper. So I just let her do all the work.

Betty was worried about anyone knowing she was in counseling.

Betty: Marcheta, I want to make sure no one knows about me coming to see you. My husband is a judge, an elected position with a high profile. He has actually received death threats for certain controversial judicial decisions. That is part of the reason why the kids and I use my maiden name.

Therapist: Betty, I will take every precaution to protect your confidentiality. Tell me more about your concerns.

Betty: It's important to Fred and me to protect our family's privacy. So, I just wanted to make sure you were aware of this. Also, Fred is just so busy, he rarely has time to spend with the kids and me.

Therapist:	How do you feel about his lack of time?
Betty:	Not good. It really makes me very angry. Brooke had always been a sickly child. She had bad allergies and needed a lot of my care. We became extremely close.

Another area of major concern for Betty centered on her intense anger toward God. She had attended church regularly before Brooke's death, a habit from childhood.

Betty:	I've questioned God at least a million times as to how He would allow this to happen to my baby. The people from my church used to come and try to talk with me, but I would get so angry at them I would run them off. They really just didn't know what to say. They would say stupid, inane things. Fred rarely went to church with the kids and me. He was always too busy, and plus he has never been religious. Brooke liked Sunday School. She and Michael both had a lot of church friends.
Therapist:	Have you gone to church since Brooke's death?
Betty:	I have tried to go twice, but when they would start singing hymns I would just lose it. The songs just seem to make me even angrier.
Therapist:	I know your pastor has tried to talk with you about this. It does seem as if you miss your relationship with the church.
Betty:	Yes, I do. It's just that there are so many questions that I have to get answers to before I can go on with my faith. Right now, I just feel empty. I have not been able to cry very much since Brooke died. This bothers me.
Therapist:	Tell me more.
Betty:	I just think I should be crying more. I really don't want to talk about this anymore right now.
Therapist:	You know that you will have to deal with this eventually.
Betty:	Just not right now. I am feeling too raw.

We were still in the information gathering stage, and I didn't want to push. Another important piece—Betty reported guilty feelings about distancing herself from her son, Michael. She and her daughter had been close, while Michael usually interacted with Fred. Michael served as a reminder of her loss.

Betty:	Every time I talk to Michael, I see Brooke and it hurts tremendously. I stay away from him. I know that he can tell.
Therapist:	Has Michael been able to talk with someone about losing his sister?
Betty:	He talks with the pastor some, but it's not enough.
Therapist:	I can give you some names of counselors that specialize in working with children. Meanwhile, you and I can work on your feelings towards Michael.
Betty:	Poor Michael. (laughs) I have also become so overprotective. Brooke was an excellent student. Michael has to struggle to get good grades. I am really smothering him, but I am just afraid that I might lose him.

On the one hand, I'm emotionally distant, on the other I hover like a mother hen.

Therapist: I think it is a natural reaction to be fearful of losing your surviving child. As parents, we believe that we are going to die before our children. Is it possible that you are being too hard on yourself?

Betty: It's just so hard. Michael is rebelling against my hold on him.

Session 3. During this session, Betty talked about Fred.

Betty: I don't even remember one time that we have actually talked about losing Brooke. He is so closed, so preoccupied with work.

Therapist: How do you handle that?

Betty: I just close myself off, too, until I explode with anger. He stares at me as if I have lost my mind. He tells me I need some help, and afterwards we just act as if nothing happened.

Therapist: How would you like him to react?

Betty: I want him to show some emotion. He acts sometimes as if Brooke did not even exist. I just want to shake him and say, "Talk to me about her. She was our daughter. Don't act as if she wasn't even here."

Therapist: I can see that this makes you feel very alone. You said there was a time when the two of you talked about everything.

Betty: Yes, that's true. All we ever talk about now is the house or what is going on with Michael.

Betty went on to say that she and Fred married in their early 30s, and she was 40 when she had the twins. They have not had a sexual relationship since Brooke's death.

Betty: I have been sleeping in Brooke's room. I'll start off in my own bedroom and then Michael will come in and lie down with Fred and me. Then I leave for Brooke's room. I haven't changed Brooke's room since she died. The maid wants to clean in there, but I really don't want anybody to touch anything. I know that's not healthy, but I want to try to hold on to her for as long as I can. Michael wants Brooke's room. He has asked me several times. Right now he is in a room on the other end of the house, He wants to be closer to his dad and me.

Therapist: Betty, what do you think you should do?

Betty: I know I should put away Brooke's stuff. My sister has offered to help. I am just not quite ready. Brooke's only been gone for a few months.

More on Betty's family background—she has a younger sister who has tried to help. Historically, Betty's family has depended on her financially. Betty worries about her elderly mother, who probably should be in a nursing home. Her mother resides in a faraway city. A younger brother lives there with her mother, but according to Betty, he is little help. Betty complains that her younger brother is spoiled and selfish. The responsibility has fallen on Betty to find affordable care for her mother. Her father died several years ago.

Betty attends occasional Compassionate Friends meetings, a group that helps with loss issues. She doesn't like going to the group because she hates having to discuss her problems in a public forum.

In subsequent individual sessions, familiar themes were revisited.

Betty: I asked Fred to help with Michael, but he never finds the time. I really got on Michael about his grades. Michael doesn't even seem as if he is trying to do well in school. I just woke up in a bad mood.

I wanted Betty to be able to recognize her grieving and pain and how it was fueling anger. I used these homework assignments to good effect:

1. Bring a photo album illustrating Brooke's life to counseling.
2. Write a letter to Brooke about how much she missed her and about the complicated feelings she was experiencing. This assignment was especially on target. Betty loved to write and had kept a personal journal for years. She had stopped making journal entries since Brooke's death.
3. Write a letter to Fred expressing her feelings of loneliness and anger.
4. Start a physical exercise program.

The final area of our work in individual counseling dealt with Betty's spiritual confusion. She felt as if God had taken her daughter away from her and couldn't tolerate hearing about the "goodness of God." What role did she want God to play in her life? Did she need a belief in a higher power? She explored these issues with me and then with her pastor.

Individual counseling had helped, and it was time to bring in Fred and Michael. I had originally suggested referring Michael to a child psychologist, but Betty wanted him included in family counseling.

Therapist: Things seem to be improving. You feel more in charge of your feelings. You're less angry with your husband and son.
Betty: I have good days and bad, which beats the hell out of all bad.
Therapist: How do you feel about bringing in Fred and Michael?
Betty: I'm ready. I have talked with Fred about coming and he says that he would.
Therapist: Let's start with the two of you. After a while, we'll bring in Michael.

Individual Counseling with Fred. 2 Sessions. Fred wanted to talk with me individually, so I scheduled two individual sessions. Fred was worried about the lack of communication in his marriage. He felt terribly alone.

Fred: I know I really don't talk that much about Brooke. It just hurts so much when I do. Betty wants to talk about her all the time, but I can't take it.
Therapist: It sounds as if the two of you have different ways of dealing with this loss.

Fred: We argue about insignificant things. I just stay away from home as
                much as possible.

Therapist: It does sound as if you wish things were better between you and
                Betty.

Fred: I do. I love her very much. I may not show it a lot, but she means
                everything to me. It has been so hard.

Conjoint Counseling with Betty and Fred, 3 Sessions. When I brought the two of them together, I wasted no time exposing how they had each tried to deal with Brooke's death. Fred complained about Betty's "inability to let Brooke go" and how much it bothered him keeping Brooke's room exactly the same, like a shrine. Betty expressed how she felt that Fred had abandoned her. She griped that he was using his work as an excuse to avoid helping her take care of Michael and the house. Two sessions devoted to serious venting! They felt better and scheduled a weekend away together. They returned from this weekend more in tune with each other and determined to communicate more.

At our third session, they got down to it and shared how much they truly missed Brooke. Fred made a decision to find more time for Betty and his family.

Individual Counseling with Michael, 2 Sessions. Michael seemed to be adjusting reasonably well. He was bringing up his grades in school and was active in sports. He talked about missing Brooke and how his mother seemed to be angry at him all the time. Also, he complained that she was always babying him. He acknowledged, however, that his mother was improving.

I encouraged Michael to talk with his school counselor. I knew this counselor, and I felt confident that he could help Michael stay out of trouble at school.

Conjoint Counseling with Betty, Fred, and Michael, 4 Sessions. I encouraged openness about grieving. I asked about the changes each family member wanted to see. I assigned communication exercises as homework.

Betty invited her sister over to the house to help her with Brooke's room. Her sister packed most of the items up and gave them to Goodwill Industries, and we got Fred to repaint the room to suit Michael. Betty had to leave the house on the day these tasks were done, but she made it through. Michael moved into the room and started sleeping on his own away from his parents' bedroom.

■ Outcome

I would judge this case as a success with a positive prediction for continued growth in family relationships. Betty continued seeing me on an occasional maintenance basis. She is enrolled in a master's program in elementary education and is tutoring in her church's community educational program.

Time heals all wounds.

■ Discussion

I was used to contracting with the Department of Human Resources and not having to handle client fees. I had a very hard time taking money from Betty! We would have an extremely emotional session, and then I had to collect my money. Eventually, I brought this out in the open and discovered that she, also, found fee-for-service uncomfortable. We agreed that she would simply leave her check with the receptionist. This cut down on my feelings of being a "mercenary" and her level of discomfort. This episode highlighted what continues to be an unpleasant aspect of private practice for me.

I had experienced several deaths of individuals close to me in the year or so before working with Betty. I was hesitant to work with her because of these recent personal losses. Could I help without allowing my personal grief to overshadow Betty's needs? I talked with a trusted colleague and was encouraged to proceed. Of course, there were times when I would become quite emotional during the sessions, but my personal losses made it possible to relate to Betty's feelings of spiritual confusion and anger. I closely monitored my reactions to make sure they weren't interfering with professional objectivity and continued to consult with my colleague. I kept myself pretty well grounded.

Biographical Statement

Marcheta Evans, Ph.D., is associate professor of counseling at the University of Texas at San Antonio. She is a licensed professional counselor in Texas. Marcheta was an associate professor in the counseling program at Auburn University at Montgomery and worked as a counselor with the Alabama Family and Juvenile Services Department. She has maintained a part-time private practice and consulting business. You may contact Marcheta at mevans@utsa.edu.

7

It's Not Our Fault

Molly Geil and William M. Walsh

Extreme distrust exists between these warring couples who share children in common. Two of the children have just been discharged from a psychiatric hospital, where they were treated for substance abuse. Fears about sexual abuse are still another complication.

This case is told from the perspective of university supervisors who head a therapeutic team. Solution-focused therapy is the team's treatment of choice, and the authors include a genogram to help the reader keep the players straight and a glossary of solution-oriented terminology.

he Phillips and Weatherford families were referred by staff at a psychiatric hospital. Once at our university clinic, the families were treated by a therapeutic team consisting of two supervisors, William Walsh and Molly Geil (who observed from behind one-way glass), and two therapists, Bob and Rebecca. William was the director of the clinic and supervising professor for the therapy sessions, and Molly was a doctoral student in training as a supervisor. This case is presented by the supervisors' voice, so "we" and "us" usually refer to William and Molly. Bob and Rebecca were completing their family counseling practicum as part of their MA program. They could choose to work in any major therapeutic model with a family.

All sessions at our clinic are videotaped. The clinic does not charge a fee, and families may be seen for as long as necessary. On the average, families are in counseling for 12 sessions.

The Phillips family consisted of Douglas, the father; Douglas's four children by Diane, his former wife—Frank, 23, Max, 18, Dennis, 14, and Darlene, 11; and Valerie, Douglas's third wife and the children's stepmother. See Figure 07-01 for a family tree.

Initially the family came to therapy because of drug abuse by all three boys. The two older boys had been in an inpatient psychiatric hospital for substance abuse, and the family was referred for family treatment after their recent discharge.

Douglas regarded his sons' drug use as the primary problem in the family. Other Phillips family members, however, complained that the family had communication problems with the biological mother, Diane, and her husband, Roy Weatherford. Sexual abuse was hinted at by several family members. Diane had custody of Dennis and

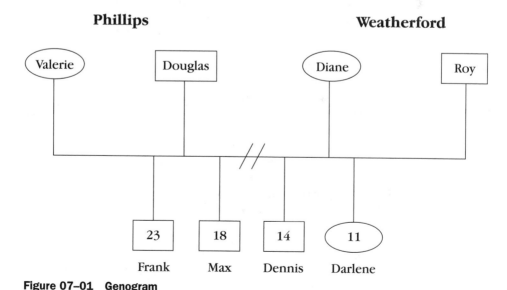

Figure 07–01   Genogram

Darlene every other Thursday evening and every other weekend. We invited Diane and Roy Weatherford to the second session.

During the intervening week, the families discussed our invitation to attend the second session together. Douglas and Diane, the biological parents, were afraid that conflict would arise if the two families were seen conjointly. We honored their decision.

So, let's set the scene. Diane and Roy (her third husband) Weatherford were seen conjointly. Douglas and Valerie (his third wife) Phillips were seen conjointly. The biological children of Diane and Douglas were usually included in the sessions with the Weatherfords. During their first session, the Weatherford family stated that their agreed-upon goal was to improve communication. Roy also wanted to discuss the welfare of the children when they were with Douglas and Valerie. He said that cooperation between families would be difficult because "Valerie would not cooperate with Diane." Roy also suspected that sexual abuse of some sort was occurring when the children were at the Phillips' house.

◼ Conceptualization

The children were caught in the middle of warring marriages. Douglas and Valerie had fought a bitter child custody battle. The biological parents told us that they had learned to communicate about the children, but the *couples* refused to be together in the same room.

Both biological parents worried about their children's substance abuse. However, Roy Weatherford did not seem concerned about Dennis's drug use. He saw it as "natural" for teenagers to experiment with drugs. Did he think it natural that the two older boys had been hospitalized for substance abuse?

Issues of sexual abuse surfaced. All three of the Phillips boys, Frank, Max, and Dennis, had been sexually abused by an uncle, Diane's brother. Diane had been abused by the same individual. She did not share this information in her family session, but her ex-husband Douglas did. Roy, Diane's current husband, had also been abused, by his father. Roy and Diane, especially, were anxious about keeping the children safe, particularly Darlene. On occasion they had found Darlene and Dennis asleep in the same bedroom, though not in the same bed, while at their house. Thus, we explored issues of sexual abuse and considered reporting of sexual abuse during the course of therapy.

Confidentiality of sessions between the two systems was another sticky issue because two of the children attended sessions with both families. Within a solution-focused format, we worked with the common presenting concerns, namely communication, drug abuse, and possible sexual abuse. The reader may want to refer to the following glossary or go directly to the source, Steve deShazer, founder of solution-focused therapy.

1. *Circular questions.* Asking a family member to comment on or speculate about another member's beliefs, feelings, or behaviors.

2. *Visitor.* A visitor attends the session but doesn't want to change anything.

3. *Complainant.* A complainant wants other people in the family to change.

4. *Customer.* A customer uses counseling to make changes.

5. *Deconstruction.* Questioning that reduces global ideas or goals to being more specific and workable.

6. *Exception question.* "When did you *not* have the problem when by all rights you should have?"

7. *Formula First Session Task (FFST).* A standard homework assignment given to the family after the first session. The FFST asks the family to observe and identify elements of their family that they do *not* want to change.

8. *Miracle question.* "Suppose one night, while you were asleep, there was a miracle and this problem was solved. How would you know?"

9. *Scaling.* Describing feelings or behaviors on a scale of 1 to 10.

In assessing the status of family members, the team concluded that the children were *visitors* even though the boys were the identified patients. Douglas Phillips was a particular challenge due to his *complainant* status. In general, many of the solutions generated by both families involved changing the behavior of the other parent (e.g., Douglas doesn't monitor the kids, they should be with us; Diane is a pathological liar). The team decided that the first step in therapy should be to work with the Weatherford family to engender more of a *customer* status. Bob and Rebecca pursued information the family provided about their relationships and asked what they would be doing differently when someone else was changing. As the Weatherford family complained about how things were in the Phillips family, Bob and Rebecca acknowledged these feelings and developed questions aimed at what Roy and Diane would be doing when things were better.

Because both families were overwhelmed by complaints, they were given the Formula First Session Task (FFST) to help identify exceptions. The FFST asked the families separately to identify what they did *not* want to change in their families. This strategy helped the families to begin to look at strengths they possessed. Circular questioning was used to help get all family members involved in identifying exceptions and family goals. A cooperative stance was maintained during the therapeutic process even when decisions were being made about the necessity of reporting sexual abuse.

Deconstruction was used to find out what the family meant by "better communication." Bob and Rebecca asked the family what it looks like when they are communicating well. Bob and Rebecca asked for specific examples of good communication in the family and who would notice first when the family is communicating better. Deconstruction was useful in helping the family better define their goals for therapy. Moreover, the family developed a clearer picture of how they would like things to be in their family.

Scaling was used frequently to find out how concerned family members were about the threats of sexual abuse and substance abuse. The Weatherford family in particular came up with specific tasks that they could do so that they would be less concerned, yet vigilant, regarding the sexual abuse issues in the family. By asking "What's different in your home since the issue of sexual abuse first came up two weeks ago?" we were able to monitor the safety of both Dennis and Darlene. If the family did not take steps to ensure the children's safety and if abuse was seen as a current threat rather than a future possibility, reporting was expressed as the solution by Molly and William.

The miracle question was used with the Weatherford family to gain insight as to how they would like things to be in their family. The team felt that it was important to work with what was possible in their miracle (e.g., The Weatherfords had custody of the kids in their miracle, so we went with, "When the kids are at your house . . .")." Also, Bob and Rebecca worked to find out the Phillipses' goals by asking how they would know when they were done with therapy.

Another strategy was "going with the resistance." Bob and Rebecca used homework, circular questioning, and looking for exceptions to point out positive things that were already occurring. These techniques helped family members become customers in the change process.

Finally, a therapeutic break was taken during sessions to formulate compliments for the family. Given the tendency of the family to carry on with complaints during session, the therapeutic break proved to be a constructive time for us to get together as a team. The families used the break as a time to "communicate," which we noted from behind the glass and later processed with the family as movement towards one of their primary goals.

Process

Early Sessions. Each of the families was seen for 11 sessions, for a total of 22 sessions over 15 weeks. The Phillips family was consistently late for sessions, which disconcerted the therapists, Bob and Rebecca. Douglas Phillips told Bob and Rebecca at the conclusion of the first session that he would be bringing the boys every other week and that his ex-wife Diane would bring the children on alternate weeks because that was their custody arrangement. It was clear to the team that Douglas was a complainant, and he believed his family's difficulties were caused by the boys. Our first goal was then to have all family members present in the sessions.

When the therapists stressed to Douglas that it was important for all family members to be present each week, he seemed to agree. However, he missed the next two sessions (his ex-wife Diane had the children both of those weeks). A shift occurred in the Phillips family when Valerie began attending. To attend the sessions with her husband and stepchildren, Valerie had to have someone cover for her at work.

Valerie: I think this is important, and I want to be here for the kids. I will try to change my schedule at work so I can be here.

Valerie's sacrifice encouraged Douglas to be more committed to attending the sessions. They continued to arrive late despite Bob and Rebecca's confrontations with the Phillips family about this issue. Douglas was the culprit. He rushed into the sessions straight from work with his cell phone activated, fielding work calls during the session.

The Weatherford family brought Dennis and Darlene to their first session, as they had custody during that week. They wanted all the adults to sit down together to discuss the children. However, the Phillips couple wouldn't go along.

Diane and Roy Weatherford were enthusiastic about the possibility that therapy could help their relationship with Dennis and Darlene. They arrived early for sessions and liked getting "homework" to do during the week. They were customers from the start.

Diane and Roy showed up alone to their second session. Dennis had refused to come, and they were not sure where Darlene was. Diane and Roy had accused Dennis of smoking marijuana earlier that afternoon, which provoked a crisis. Diane began to cry and explained to the therapists that each of her sons had been sexually abused by her brother. Roy added that he had been sexually abused by his father. After the break, Roy reported to the therapists that he was concerned about Dennis's behavior toward Darlene. Dennis and Darlene had occasionally slept in the same bedroom at Roy and Diane's house. Roy and Diane had no evidence of sexual activity and hadn't confronted the kids about it. For the remainder of the session, Bob and Rebecca explored with Diane and Roy solutions they had for keeping Darlene safe. Because of the unclear and inconclusive nature of the situation, we (William and Molly) suggested to Bob and Rebecca that they should question the family further about these incidents of sleeping together before reporting to the Department of Social Services.

Bob and Rebecca explained to Roy and Diane that they were obligated both legally and ethically to report any incidents of suspected or known child abuse. The therapy team wanted to seek a collaborative solution to the sexual abuse issue. They asked the couple for their help in determining what steps should be taken by the team. Bob and Rebecca stressed the importance of keeping Darlene safe. The Weatherfords agreed. They suggested that Douglas and Valerie should be notified about the situation at the Weatherfords' house and questioned about what was happening at their own home. Then Darlene was invited into the session. The team believed Darlene when she said that nothing sexual was going on between her and her brother Dennis.

Diane said she would talk to Dennis individually. She also would share with Darlene materials she had on ways to keep safe from abuse. She would stop them from sleeping in the same room. Roy would conduct bed checks.

During an early session with the Phillips family, Bob and Rebecca disclosed the Weatherfords' worries about Dennis and Darlene sleeping in the same room (permission to disclose had been obtained). Douglas and Valerie reported that Dennis and Darlene never slept in the same room at their house. Douglas asked that Dennis not be confronted about sexual abuse because it would make Dennis mad.

Despite Douglas's request, Bob and Rebecca later questioned Dennis about sleeping with Darlene. Dennis explained that because his mom makes the kids go to bed "really early," at eight o'clock, they get bored and lonely and "just talk at night" until they fall asleep. The team was satisfied that there were no indications of sexual abuse that warranted reporting.

Because this was Valerie's first session, and she appeared to be willing to make some changes herself, she was given the FFST of listing what she did not want to change in the family.

After that second session, Bob and Rebecca expressed doubt about the solution-focused approach as applied to such serious problems as sexual and drug abuse. They told us, their supervisors, about their urge to be more direct about dangerous issues. We assured Bob and Rebecca that the solution-focused model did not require them to be circumspect about sexual abuse. We advised them to stick with the solution-focused approach.

Fortunately, soon after this difficult discussion, Bob and Rebecca were pleasantly surprised that staying in their model had helped the Weatherford family to make significant gains. Diane had followed through with talking to Darlene and Dennis, and she felt positive about her communication with her children. Roy conducted bed checks, and he also moved the bedrooms so that his and Diane's bedroom was between Dennis's room and Darlene's room. Diane and Roy had demonstrated teamwork during the past week by establishing rules and consequences for the family. They discovered that conflict and stress in their family had lessened.

The miracle question was then posed to the Weatherfords to determine what things they would like to see different in their family. Roy and Diane's miracle included them having custody of Dennis and Darlene. Knowing that this was not a possibility via therapy, Bob and Rebecca chose to focus on something else that Roy and Diane had said, that she wanted to regain "that loving family feeling" they had when the kids were living with them. Bob and Rebecca deconstructed with the family what they would need to do to recreate this feeling. They used scaling to gauge where Roy and Diane currently saw their family, and they asked each person what he or she could do to move up just one number on the scale. Roy stated that he would have to talk and snuggle more. Diane added that she would need to be more supportive and less critical of Roy.

Because time was short in the session, the therapists gave the couple the task of doing more of whatever they believed would move them up on the scale. Therapy was shifting away from the children and toward the marital relationship.

Middle Sessions. While the Weatherford family became customers, the Phillips family remained as visitors and complainants through the early sessions. Of course, the team wanted to move Valerie and Douglas toward customer status. Douglas continued to complain about his ex-wife, and he thought he had to do something about his sons' drug problems. He pushed for drug testing. He became angry, stating he felt "set up" when the therapists wanted him to listen without interrupting. Although Douglas said he wanted to work on communicating with his sons, he was blind to his responsibility in shutting down interaction. Bob and Rebecca were anxious to have Douglas do something different. When Bob and Rebecca came up with solutions, Douglas resisted. We suggested to Bob and Rebecca that they stop giving suggestions and instead provide Douglas with easy homework assignments until he was ready to do something different.

By the middle sessions, Bob and Rebecca felt hopeful about the Weatherfords' progress. They saw the sessions shifting to focus more on the couple's relationship when they came without the children. When the Weatherfords attended with the children, the focus of therapy was again the family. Diane wanted to increase communication with her children. Roy wanted better communication too, but added that the family needed to give him more respect. Dennis and Darlene both said they would like to do more fun things as a family. Instead of deconstructing communication and looking at family time as a solution, Bob and Rebecca focused on "the problem" of communication in the family. During the break, we (Molly and William) suggested a family task: to observe times when the family communicated well.

The Weatherfords continued to progress. Roy was watching less TV and spending more time with the family.

Diane: I know Roy is trying, and I don't feel the need to criticize him.
Roy: We did have an interesting discussion about religion this week with the kids.

Diane wanted to take the kids bowling during the coming week. Roy thought this was too expensive. They successfully negotiated to keep the cost down.

While the Weatherford family was solving problems, the Phillips family continued to come late to sessions. Bob and Rebecca were anxious that each week would bring more complaining from Douglas. They decided to address Dennis and Darlene first because they had been engaged in the sessions with the Weatherfords. Rebecca asked Darlene what was different this week, and she stated proudly that she had made a dinner for the family. The other family members were asked the same question.

Dennis: (bowing his head as usual) I don't know.
Valerie: (quickly) His grades are improving, and he received a 100% on his algebra test.

Dennis smiled at the compliment. We noted from behind the glass that it was the first time we'd seen him smile.

Valerie: Darlene and I are talking more.

Darlene agreed.

After each of the other family members talked about how things were improving, Douglas contributed to the conversation.

Douglas: I am going to try to come home for dinner more often.

Valerie looked surprised. Bob and Rebecca came into the observation room for their session break excited about the possibility that Douglas was becoming a customer. Returning to the session, they deconstructed with Douglas how he would accomplish his goal. He was told to try to make it home for dinner this week, but only one time. Bob warned Douglas that any more than that might be too difficult to start with. Despite his stated commitment, Douglas was 20 minutes late to the next session. When Rebecca asked what was different this week, Valerie and Douglas said that, although they tried to arrange a family dinner, they were "unable to connect." Douglas was late so everyone began eating without him.

Later Sessions. Although the bowling event was fun, Roy Weatherford was discouraged when he and Diane came without the children. He believed his relationship with Diane was not good, and he was concerned about the family's finances. Roy added that he was tired of them always focusing on the children, and he wished that he and Diane could focus on each other. Diane said that things with the kids were good. She thought Roy was down due to his approaching birthday and added that he "always gets like this at birthdays."

Bob normalized Roy's feeling of taking a step backward, noting that this was common in therapy. Rebecca and Bob also explained that in families with children, children are often the first focus in therapy. However, in later stages of therapy, the couple begins to focus on themselves, and things may appear to become worse. Rebecca confessed that she and Bob had been sucked into Roy's depressed mood.

Bob and Rebecca were struggling, because in earlier sessions the family had made many positive changes in their interactions with their children. We suggested that Bob and Rebecca return to a first-session format of asking the couple for a new statement of complaints, deconstruction, and looking for exceptions. The Weatherford family did not show up for their next session. The team suspected that it was in part due to the shift in focus from the children to the couple relationship. Roy wanted to move in that direction, but Diane was hesitant.

At this point, Bob and Rebecca were discouraged about the progress that both families were making in therapy. They decided to ask the Phillips family how they would know that they no longer needed to come to therapy. Dennis said he would be spending more time with the family, something he had asked for from Diane and Roy, also. Valerie said she would be more patient, particularly with Darlene. Douglas stated that he would be angry less often and use a calmer tone of voice with the children. Max, who hadn't been to therapy since the first session, continuously smirked and even laughed when Douglas spoke about his commitment to changing things for himself. Max seemed to be under the influence of drugs in the session. Bob confronted Max about his reaction.

Max: I don't think he is as committed as he says he is.

Rebecca and Bob asked the family to notice the first small sign that others were doing something different. After the session, the team discussed Max's comment about Douglas. They believed that Douglas was critical to change in the family and was not a customer. Everyone in the family has discussed spending more time together, but everyone also noted how busy Douglas's schedule is and that he is often late for things. We (William and Molly) suggested that Bob and Rebecca needed to engage the system in doing things together with or without Douglas. If the team's hypothesis was correct, Douglas would join in because he had demonstrated all along that he did not like to be left out of anything.

The next session brought a breakthrough for the Phillips family. Douglas was again late to the session. The therapists elected to begin the session with Valerie.

Valerie stated that her goal for the family remained the same, that she wanted to work on "better communication." Douglas entered the room at that point, and he immediately began to fulfill his role as the complainant. He stated that he knew the boys were using drugs, and he was going to have them drug tested. Shortly before the break, Douglas seemed to shift toward doing something different.

Valerie:	I feel it is important to spend more time together as a family.
Douglas:	I want to focus on the boys' drug use. I feel we need to have them drug tested.
Bob:	What can you do to help the boys from turning to drugs?
Douglas:	I think I need to spend more time with them.
Rebecca:	On a scale of 1 to 10, with 1 being you spend no time at all with the boys and 10 being you spend as much time as you'd like with them, where are you right now?
Douglas:	About a two.
Rebecca:	What do you need to do to spend just a little more time with the boys? Move from a two to a three, say.
Douglas:	They refuse and act disinterested when I ask them to do stuff with me.

At this point Douglas reeled off several complaints. Bob and Rebecca asked Valerie circular questions about times when she saw Douglas and Dennis spending time together. Valerie offered some examples of times when Dennis was more engaged with the family. She talked about times when they were all together as a family. At the break, the team suggested that Douglas and Valerie be assigned the task of getting Dennis more engaged in the family. When Rebecca and Bob gave this task, Douglas immediately responded.

Douglas:	The drug testing will get him engaged. It may not be positive, but at least it will get his attention and get him engaged.
Rebecca:	(going with the resistance) What if the drug tests are positive? What can each of you do to help the other from becoming discouraged?
Valerie:	I can be more supportive of Douglas. I will back Douglas up over the kids.
Douglas:	(breaking down and crying) Valerie doesn't need to back me up or support me because I never take a stand for her to support. I have always been so wishy-washy with the boys. (crying harder) It is my fault that my kids are using drugs because I have never set any limits.

Douglas and Valerie decided to call drug treatment centers and talk about what to do if the tests were positive. They also agreed to spend more time together as a family. During the next session, Douglas kept hammering away on drug testing. The team asked the miracle question: "What would it be like if Douglas were suddenly able to follow through and take a stand?" Douglas responded that a drug test would solve everything.

Dennis:	I guess if he takes a definite stand, I would have to take a drug test.

Roy used a metaphor of a wall between him and Diane. Bob and Rebecca worked on how Roy and Diane could remove the wall, one brick at a time. Roy realized that he needed to share his worries more with Diane, and Diane thought she could help Roy by listening without being critical or trying to solve his problems for him. When the kids were with Roy and Diane, the focus shifted to family communication. During the session, the family had a disagreement over something that had happened that week and the team complimented the family on their ability to communicate about a difficult issue. This positive reframe encouraged more communication.

Roy: I had thought we were having a fight, but I do think that Diane was listening.
Bob: Does communication include always agreeing with each other?
Diane: No, at least we are talking. But I need to be less critical of Roy. It is hard.
Roy: I didn't shut down like I usually do.

A shift occurred in the Phillips family during the next session when the family was asked what was different. Darlene and Valerie said that the family had dinner a couple of times together. All the team members noticed that Dennis had on a white T-shirt that week and was not wearing his hat. When Bob commented on this difference, Dennis smiled. Douglas again said he was concerned about the boys' drug use and thought he should have them drug tested. The therapists decided to review the homework asking Douglas to take a stand.

Douglas: I don't know. I feel that I do let little things slide, but I take a stand with more serious issues.
Valerie: That's true.
Rebecca: I am confused. You just stated that you take a stand on more serious issues. Each week you have told us that Dennis's drug use is a very serious concern for you, yet you have not fulfilled your commitment to have Dennis drug tested. (silence)
Douglas: I don't know what to do with the results.
Rebecca: Dennis, what do you think your dad could do in the meantime to reduce his fears about your using drugs?
Dennis: Trust me more.
Rebecca: What can you do to help your dad trust you more?

Dennis was unsure, so Rebecca asked Valerie what she thought he might do. Valerie said that Dennis could come out of his basement room and spend more time with the family in the evening. Dennis thought he could do that but said his computer was in the basement, and he used it a lot in the evenings. But he added that he would try.

Darlene came in with Diane and Roy the following week. Diane and Roy had been arguing and were very angry. Roy read a poem that he had written to the family about feeling unloved and not included. The response was positive. Darlene said she would hug Roy more. Diane was going to show affection to Roy by surprising him with things, and she would do an activity with Roy during the week. Roy said he would be less selfish, but Bob and Rebecca did not deconstruct "selfish" or push Roy about what he would do differently. On the way out, Roy noted that they had only one more session.

Roy: (to Bob) After next week, what are you going to do . . . you throw us out to the wolves?

It was clear that Roy did not feel that their work was done. However, the family therapy clinic was closing for the summer.

Douglas attended the Phillips family session alone the next week because Valerie was sick. Before coming in, Douglas had asked Valerie what was different this week. She said she thought Dennis was trying to be with the family more, and that he and Max seemed more friendly to Douglas. Douglas said he thought this was because he was following through with specific consequences more and not being as pushy. Douglas also said that, for his part, he had made arrangements to spend more time with the family. He scheduled family dinners in his planner. Rebecca and Bob asked Douglas circular questions to involve other family members. Douglas believed that Valerie was surprised when he had shown up for dinner.

Bob asked Douglas what he thought he had gained from therapy. The following dialogue between Douglas and Bob solidified for the team that Douglas had become a customer in the process.

Douglas: One thing I am noticing is that my actions or nonactions have affected my family. It has been good that I have made time to come home for dinner. I think it would be great to get the kids more involved in some activities, and I would like to do more with them. I still think that follow-through is a problem for me. I think the drug test would take care of that.

Bob: It seems that your family really enjoys spending more time with you, and that has created some positive changes for everyone. What are some things that you could do to spend more time with the boys?

Douglas: I could work on the computer with Dennis. I also have been talking more to the kids so that they feel more comfortable with me.

Bob: Oh, talking more to them. That is different for you.

Douglas: Yes it is, and I think it may be why Valerie sees the boys being more friendly to me. You know, I was thinking that I could ask Dennis and Max what they would like to do to get them more involved.

Bob: Sure, why not ask them?

The session ended with the team giving Douglas the task of doing something different over the next week but not telling anyone what he was doing. He seemed to like that idea, as evidenced by his smile and comment: "I think I can do that." Rebecca later commented to Molly that she and Bob believed Douglas would complete his task and that it would be the first time he had followed through.

__Termination.__ The last session for the Weatherford family began with Roy and Diane stating that they felt things were different in the last week. Diane said Roy had been trying to communicate his feelings more, and she believed she was able to listen to Roy without being critical. Roy said he felt more comfortable talking to Diane since he had gotten some of his feelings out.

Overall, the couple believed they were making headway in their relationship, even though they knew that they had some work to do. They spoke of taking the summer off and returning to the clinic in the fall. Diane believed their relationship with Dennis and Darlene had been much improved. Bob and Rebecca spoke with the couple about how they would maintain some of the changes they had made and warned them about occasional relapses.

When Bob and Rebecca opened the last session with the Phillips family by asking what had been different the past week, everyone responded. Valerie immediately said that Douglas had been consistently coming home for dinner with the family, and that she had really enjoyed having dinner as a family. Douglas chuckled and said that is what he had done for homework, but he did not think anyone had noticed. Darlene and Dennis saw their dad as setting more limits, particularly with Darlene. Then they reported that the family had decided to take a trip this summer, something they had not done in the past few years.

When asked about the gains they had made in therapy, Valerie noticed that spending more time as a family led naturally to greater communication. She believed that continuing to spend family time together would help meet her goal of better communication. Douglas realized that spending time with the family was important, and he vowed to continue his efforts to do so. Dennis added that he thought family time was important for better communication, and he offered to bring his computer upstairs so he could be with the family even when he was working on the computer. Darlene said that she enjoyed coming to therapy because her family always went out to dinner together after the sessions, and "it was fun."

Before the end of the session, Douglas responded to Rebecca's question regarding maintenance of change: "You know I need to work at being more patient with the kids and being with them at home. I don't want to slack off by thinking that everything is better for us now. I know I'll need to keep working at it." Rebecca and Bob wished the family a good summer and told them not to hesitate to call in the fall if new issues came up for them.

◾ Outcome

Both families made positive changes. Despite the fact that the couples did not come to therapy together, Douglas and Diane—the children's biological parents—exchanged phone calls. Initially, Douglas said the problems their children were having were Diane's fault. Roy and Diane complained about a bitter custody battle with Douglas and thought he got what he deserved. Given the complainant status of all of the adults in the system, we judged ourselves successful in that each of the adults became an honest customer during the course of therapy. Bob and Rebecca facilitated both families in changing the focus from the identified problem of drug abuse to systemwide issues such as family communication, time together, and couple issues.

Changes were noticed by the Weatherford family in their relationships with the children as well as their relationship as a couple. The success experienced by the Weatherford family in defusing the troublesome abuse issues with Dennis and Darlene may have trickled over to the Phillips family. Darlene and Dennis both became more involved in the therapy process. The changes were particularly evident for Dennis, and he shared his ideas about the family. It was symbolic of this growth that he wore all black with a baseball cap pulled over his eyes to the initial visits but white T-shirts without the baseball cap to the final two sessions. Dennis began to make eye contact with the therapists and smile more. As pieces of the system began to shift, both family systems experienced change. Dennis and Darlene facilitated workable solutions for both families when they asked to spend more time with their parents and stepparents.

The major shift for the Phillips family came toward the end of therapy. When Douglas became a customer and began to make small changes, the family became more positive. As noted by Rebecca and Bob after the first session, Douglas held significant power in the family. Douglas's change created a change in his perception about who is responsible for change in a family. During the last two sessions with the Phillips family, Douglas did not mention drug testing for his sons. He focused more on positive changes the family had made, although he was still concerned about drug use. Douglas recognized solutions that helped his family function better, and he even scheduled a family vacation so that, as he put it, "We could have some time together as a family."

It will be difficult for the Phillips family to maintain changes if Douglas does slack off, as he said he might. Douglas's spending time with his family seemed to be an important issue for the family. Because Dennis and Max are teenagers, they may resist spending time with their dad. We believed that what Dennis really wanted was attention from his dad. If Douglas can keep their time together focused in a positive way, they may develop a more trusting relationship. It appeared to the team that Max was involved with drugs, as his father stated. Dennis's behavior was unclear, and he seemed to become increasingly invested in therapy. It is hoped that Douglas can remain focused on the positive things Dennis does. The Weatherford family will likely maintain some of the changes they made in therapy because they were customers in the process. Their challenge will be to continue to communicate as a couple and recognize that they have more work they can do. They will likely return to therapy in the fall, based on Roy's commitment to making changes in their relationship and his recognition that they had only begun to scratch the surface of some important issues in their relationship (e.g., finances).

■ Discussion

The team thought that the results of this case were positive, given the tough presenting problems and the tendency of all of the adults to blame others. One issue that was a surprise for the team, however, was the sexual abuse issue that came up in the second session with the Weatherford family. It was reported that Darlene and Dennis were spending time in their bedrooms together after they were sent to bed.

Consistent with solution-focused family therapy, the therapists guided the families in developing their own solutions to this concern (e.g., the kids were more closely supervised, Douglas and Diane spoke over the telephone regarding the matter). The therapy team believed that nothing sexual was going on between Dennis and Darlene, and did not take further action. It was only after the concern about sexual abuse was resolved that the families stopped complaining about each other and became focused on issues of concern within their family system. When the family members were able to develop solutions, the therapy team noted that the family began to perceive themselves as capable of resolving daily issues.

At termination the team felt good about the accomplishments the Phillips family had made and sent them off with the task of doing more of what they had been doing. The team also felt positive about the changes that the Weatherford family had made. However, Bob and Rebecca believed the Weatherfords would benefit from future therapy focusing on Diane and Roy as a couple. Diane and Roy were provided with referral sources in case they decided to continue counseling. We all believed they would likely come back to the clinic in the fall to continue their work together.

The four team members enjoyed working together. We (the supervisors) assumed ultimate responsibility for the treatment, so there was a clear hierarchical arrangement in decision making. However, all discussions took place in an atmosphere of equality and collaboration, and all team members believed they had input to decisions. This mind-set precluded issues of competition and jealousy that can infect therapeutic teams. We pushed the therapists to apply the methods of solution-focused therapy, knowing that they are free to accept or reject this approach in their future practice. In fact, Bob and Rebecca are working in community mental health settings and report that they are using solution-focused techniques.

Biographical Statement

Molly Geil, Ph.D., received her doctorate in school psychology from the University of Northern Colorado. She is an adjunct professor in the Division of Professional Psychology at UNC, and she supervises interns in local school districts. Molly consults with families and international schools in Seoul, South Korea. You can reach her at mollyg02@aol.com.

William M. Walsh, Ph.D., is a professor in the Division of Professional Psychology and director of family therapy at the University of Northern Colorado. He supervised and coordinated the team that worked with the Phillips and Weatherford families. Bill's research, publications, and consulting focus on the creative applications of systems theory. His latest books are *Essentials of Family Therapy, 2nd edition* (2002) and *Schools and Family Therapy* (1997). You can reach Bill at william.walsh@unco.edu.

8

Let Me Be Me

Joshua M. Gold

Joshua Gold uses a structural–strategic model to assist a family struggling with adolescent challenges to parental wisdom and authority. Therapy is successful but not in the way that Gold planned. He underestimated parental attachment to family-of-origin child-rearing style. Gold successfully changes therapeutic horses in midstream and adds in family scripting. He asks himself, "How should I explain a strategic error to my clients?"

T he Taylor family self-referred to me not because the parents saw themselves in trouble but because of what they labeled the hypersensitivity of son Steven, 10, and the "aloofness" of daughter Kevin, 14. Kevin's conflict style exacerbated her brother's extreme emotionalism. The parents had hoped that Steven would outgrow his emotionalism, but the number and severity of his eruptions were getting worse. The father, Tim, 38, was more upset by Steven's outbursts than was the mother, Mary, 37. For her part, Mary worried about Kevin's demands for privacy. She was angry about Kevin's refusal to even talk to her.

Tim and Mary grew up in the same rural community and noticed each other in high school, where Mary was a cheerleader and Tim played football, basketball, and baseball. They attended the same university and each earned a degree in business administration. Tim majored in accounting and Mary in banking. Both were employed in their chosen careers and had worked for the same company since college graduation. Both marital partners described their lives as pleasant, their marriage as satisfying, and their relationships with their children and family-of-origin as close. Both Kevin (named after Tim's grandfather) and Steven (named after Mary's father) were described as bright, polite children, "doing as they are told," and "fun to be with."

The parents wanted Kevin to be more communicative and enthusiastic about an upcoming family vacation. Mary wanted to be closer to Kevin, just as she and her mother were best friends at this difficult stage in life. Both parents wanted Steven to become more mature.

When I worked with this family, I was an assistant professor of marriage and family therapy at the University of South Carolina. Our program was experimenting with teaching methods to make family theory more real for students. As part of my instruction of a 15-week family theory course, I wanted students to observe family counseling. To recruit families, I had offered my services at two community agencies for 10 sessions of free family counseling, on the condition that I could refer the most severe cases to other clinicians. The Taylor family responded to my offer and agreed to being observed by my graduate students.

■ Conceptualization

If I had to decide on a diagnosis for Steven, as the identified patient, I would classify him as having a mood disorder. His crying episodes interfered with socialization, and I saw no age-appropriate verbal communication skills. If I had consulted with the parents about a diagnosis for Kevin, I imagine that they would label her behavior as oppositional defiant disorder, with reference to loss of temper, arguing with adults, and irritability. In my opinion, Kevin's behavior wasn't developmentally inappropriate, but from her parents' perspective, the emerging defiance was totally unacceptable.

Given the time limit of one semester for treatment, I initially opted for a structural–strategic approach. From that perspective, Steven could be ineffectually attempting to communicate his individual preferences to his father and enlisting his mother's support in the attempt. His outbursts also served a detouring function by diverting attention from the escalating conflict between Kevin and their parents. I saw Kevin as trying to create personal privacy and an identity independent from that expected by her parents. Kevin's conflict style demanded that the parents learn to negotiate with this noncompliant individual.

From a structural–strategic viewpoint, my goals were to (1) ally Tim and Mary so they would not be divided by the children and would collaborate on meeting their children's needs; (2) create clear boundaries to replace the diffuse boundaries between the parental and sibling subsystems; and (3) rebalance power as appropriate to the early adolescent developmental stage. I was convinced that increased parental respect for Kevin's individualism would result in improved communication between Kevin and her parents.

To achieve these goals, I intended to use sculpting, reframing, enactment, circular questioning, and directing. I planned to use family sculpting to illustrate the appropriate emotional distances between individuals and subsystems. I would seat the parents side by side to emphasize the need for alliance. I would separate Kevin and Steven from the parents and from each other so that the uniqueness of each child could be visibly experienced.

Reframing would change the parents' perceptions of Steven from weak, immature, and babyish to seeing him as someone with something important to say but unsure of how to get his message across. I wanted to reframe their negative view of Kevin to see her moving towards adulthood although unsure of how to communicate that new status. I wanted to change Kevin's view of her parents' behaviors from intrusive to loving attempts to provide her with guidance. Finally, I wished to reframe the parents' view of themselves as incompetent to bravely experimenting with new styles of interaction.

Enactments are replays of family conflict in which I act as director to take the interactions beyond the point where they broke down. Enactments can offset the family's negative cognitive presentation styles. I wanted to present the *affective* components of the family conflict style, an aspect omitted from the concise, logical description offered by the parents.

I used circular questioning to emphasize the unique perspective of each family member, to encourage listening and respect of differing viewpoints, and to begin the practice of family negotiation and accommodation.

My directives were intended to offer family members a new experience of each other as each acted in accordance with the command.

To the above mix of interventions, I added a solution-oriented, present focus, emphasizing behavioral improvement both in the session and through homework assignments.

However, for this family, I was moving far too quickly. The parents soon realized that they were being asked to parent in a style that they had never personally experienced. Tim and Mary disclosed that what was being offered was so discrepant from their own strict upbringing that the new style seemed artificial. They turned out okay, so why try anything else? These parents demanded proof that the new style would be effective before they experimented.

I replaced my present-oriented, action-focused goals with family-of-origin exploration and subsequent connection to current parental belief systems and modes of interaction. These parents used an idealized memory of the parenting they had received as a pattern or cookie cutter and expected ideal results. I explained our change of direction and acknowledged that the new parenting styles I had been advocating may have seemed foreign, and I wondered out loud what their upbringing had really been like. Tim and Mary wanted their children to be there during this "excavation" as a learning process.

We did not have time to create a full genogram, but we did explore the family legacy, the sanctions regarding differentiation, and gender role scripting. Family legacy refers to Tim and Mary's memories of what it meant to be members of their families, as distinct from other families, and what traditions and rituals defined their families. Sanctions regarding differentiation entailed a review of emotional penalties inflicted on family members who deviated from family-prescribed roles and behaviors. Gender role scripting exposed beliefs and actions appropriate for males and females, how those expectations were communicated, and the family response to an individual's experimentation with family-censured behaviors or attitudes.

I asked Tim and Mary how knowledge of their own upbringing was helping them understand their own child-rearing practices. I also asked Steven and Kevin what they had learned about their parents.

■ Process

The family met weekly for nine 1-hour sessions. The description of process can be divided into the first four sessions and the final five sessions.

The First Four Sessions. In the initial stage of meeting the family, the parents repeatedly spoke for the children. Even questions directed to a child by name were answered by a parent. In Session 1, Kevin crossed her arms, sat against the back of the couch she shared with her father, and stared at the floor, while Steven sat close to his mother, closed his eyes, and pretended to be asleep. Oblivious, the parents continued to expound on their disappointments with each child throughout the interview. The second session began with Tim speaking for the family and defining their problems, generating a spontaneous enactment:

Tim:	I'm sick and tired of his crying. At baseball practice last night, the coach yelled at him for missing a grounder, he threw his glove down and walked over to me saying that he quit. If I had ever done that, my father would have shown me the fence.
Mary:	Tim, you're too hard on Steven. He's trying his best. He needs more help from you, not criticism. (Mom is sitting next to Steven, across from Dad and Kevin. She puts her arm around Steven.)
Kevin:	The two of you always fuss about Steven. Why can't you just leave him alone?

Tim: You're a fine one to talk. Every time we want to talk to you, you either sit with your head down or go into your room and close the door. We can't even hold a decent conversation anymore.

Kevin: But that's the point! Why should I bother telling you what's going on with me when you never really listen?

Mom: Kevin, I really want us to be closer, but you are too angry right now for me to talk to. Maybe when you calm down, we will be able to talk like adults. (At this point, Steven begins to complain of an upset stomach. Dad looks at him disapprovingly, Mom pulls Steven closer, Kevin shakes her head and sits back in her chair with her arms crossed. An uneasy calm descends, and the family members look to the counselor.)

The pattern evident in this sequence seemed straightforward. Helping the parents learn better listening skills and accept the uniqueness of each child seemed an appropriate objective. I had success in improving communication in session, as the parents could, under my direction, ask appropriate questions, support the uniqueness of each child, and respond to each child in ways congruent with developmental level and needs. However, they failed to communicate effectively between sessions via the homework tasks. The parents complained that the directives seemed artificial, that they forgot what they were supposed to try, and that even when they did try, the children did not respond as they were supposed to. Kevin retorted that she was trying as hard as she could, but that she got so angry she just didn't care and wanted away from the family. Steven said that he was too young to do anything about it. These declarations provoked another enactment with a pattern similar to the previous one, ending with each member feeling disappointed in each other.

I wondered if my homework tasks were too confusing. However, the parents could repeat and explain what was expected. While they could parent well for brief periods of time, they could not transcend or improvise on the script from the most recent session. They were well educated and well-read, so I was puzzled as to what dynamics were interfering.

I realized that I had not considered the historical, family-of-origin issues that Tim and Mary brought to their parenting styles. I reconceptualized the Taylor case from a family-of-origin perspective. Doing so required more attention to parental insight and less attention to behavioral change. From this transgenerational orientation, I attended to the parents' differentiation between their family-of-origin (in this case from parental roles in those families) and legacies and how different a child may be from what one's parents expected yet still be assured of the parents' love and support. I used two main themes throughout this foursession exploration: (1) In your growing up at home, how did you learn what was okay or not okay for males and females? (2) When you became a teenager, how did you respond to your parents' still telling you how to be?

I initiated this exploration in Session 4 by asking about given names.

Therapist: Tell me the history of how children are named in your family. (I was especially curious about the legacy of Kevin's name.)

Tim:	We name children after family members who have passed on.
Therapist:	Kevin, what is the source of your name, and what do you know about the previous Kevin?
Kevin:	I was named after my dad's granddad. He was in the Army and died fighting for what he believed.
Therapist:	Kevin, what else do you know?
Kevin:	He was very strong and independent—always knew his mind and spoke it. He took good care of his troops. From what I heard, it's his bravery that got him killed.
Therapist:	Tim, what was your experience as Kevin's grandson?
Tim:	He was hard to get close to, I knew that I could always depend on him, and when he took a stand he never backed down. He was held up to me as the best kind of man, never complaining, doing his duty, independent, and tough.
Therapist:	Admirable qualities. How would you have liked him to be easier to get close to?
Tim:	I would have liked him to listen to me. He spent a lot of time teaching me how to be, but I never really got the sense he knew me. It's like all the grandsons got the same lessons. Well, maybe if he were still alive when I became an adult, we could have become friends.
Therapist:	You wish he had listened to you.
Tim:	Yeah. My dad was exactly the same. I knew that he loved me and wanted the best for me, but he never seemed to want my opinion on anything. When I became a teenager, we fought constantly and he threatened to throw me out. I remember to this day him standing with the door open saying, "Under my roof, my rules. They're good enough for everyone else. If you think you're too good for those rules, then get out!"
Therapist:	Those episodes sound frightening to me. When I hear that story, you seem really angry towards him.
Tim:	Yeah, but we never talk now, so being angry doesn't do me any good. He'd never want to hear it anyway, so I just stopped trying.

The Final Five Sessions. Sessions 5 through 8 followed the same theme, with input from Tim and Mary on their childhood and adolescent experiences. Both adults acknowledged the pressure they felt to conform and how confined each felt by the rigid gender roles in their families, yet each admitted that they felt secure, certain of what was acceptable to their families. Mary summed up her experience by saying, "I always felt so sure of how to get my mom and dad's love. I didn't realize how much I missed out on and compromised for their affection."

Session 9 had been contracted at the onset as the final session. I asked each family member to share what each had learned. They believed that they had learned to evaluate behavior and how to facilitate or sabotage interaction. Family members commented on how good it felt to listen and be heard. The children appreciated the insight into what they had previously seen as their parents' "perfect" childhoods, and the parents admitted that they had forgotten the more restrictive aspects of their childhood and adolescence. As of this writing, I have received no request to continue counseling or any indication that they've resumed counseling with anyone else.

Outcome

The sessions were successful but not in the manner that I had planned. The parents did communicate more directly with the children and did form a stronger parental coalition. This new style of interacting prevented marital conflict. Tim and Mary's mutual support and cooperation prevented Kevin from playing one parent against the other and allowed each parent to feel supported by the other. The children voiced appreciation for being able to state their views, although they were not pleased that their opinions were not always the ones ultimately chosen. Sharing histories opened everyone's eyes to the impact of family-of-origin experiences on current dynamics.

In contrast, the reframing of Kevin and Steven's behaviors as ineffective attempts at communication and the presentation of knowledge confirming the developmental appropriateness of Kevin's distancing from the family were unsuccessful. I am uncertain whether the parents' perceptions of their children's behavior became more lenient and accepting. I think Tim and Mary were still too enmeshed in the lives of their children, given the ages of the children and the accompanying developmental family and individual tasks. Much of the gender and role scripting—the legacies from the parents' families of origin—had not been addressed. While this process of reflection had begun, I am not optimistic that Tim and Mary will continue to review family-of-origin scripting and evaluate its contribution to current parenting without my directives.

Discussion

I wanted Tim and Mary to accept Kevin's distancing from the family as a normal, albeit unpleasant, aspect of adolescent development. They apparently bought my formulation, but they didn't do their homework. They were baffled about their own lack of follow-through and wondered aloud why my directives, which seemed so simple when demonstrated and rehearsed in session, could not be replicated at home. I sensed the possible emergence of a power struggle were I to disregard the seriousness of their inquiry and push for further behavioral change. I resolved this concern by normalizing their difficulty, suggesting that some clients learn through action, and others prefer to understand completely before they act. Both parents admitted their analytic preference to understand *why* before trying it. This discussion set the stage for our productive family-of-origin exploration.

For me, a question emerges about a change in clinical direction. How can counselors explain that shift to clients? If we propose that we made an initial error in judgment, what effect might that admission have on the clients' faith in our new focus? If we do not explain, are we "infantilizing" our clients, communicating that we can do what we will, regardless of their sense of puzzlement at our inconsistencies?

My response to these questions would be to openly acknowledge that what we first thought may be helpful now seems not so. While we all tried to use that original plan, what is more important than adherence to a plan is taking the time to evaluate its efficacy in light of its anticipated outcome and having the humility to admit when a change is needed. Any therapeutic strategy is an experiment subject to scrutiny. Such an approach on my part offers modeling for the family.

The progress in this case called for me to reconsider the issue of *structural determinism*. I understand that term to refer to the degree of change that is possible in a family without threatening the ingredients that make up that family's identity. The moment I suggested that more emotional distance from the children and the family of origin may strengthen the family, all members looked at the idea as heretical. Closeness is one of the distinguishing factors of the Taylor family's identity. Supporting Kevin's distancing challenged a core family belief. On the contrary, I needed to support closeness as strength if I was to continue working with the family.

This family taught me how important it is to integrate family history/scripting into my counseling. Tim and Mary's family histories inculcated the belief that the imposition of expectations from parent to child and a child's obedience demonstrated love. While developmentally appropriate for young children, adolescence requires a shift to a negotiation of role expectations that contributes to the adolescent's self-definition.

The question for me as a counselor is, "How can I change such core beliefs?" I don't think it's enough to ask my clients to just take my word that a new belief will be more functional!

Biographical Statement

Joshua M. Gold, Ph.D., NCC, is an associate professor in the Counselor Education program, Department of Educational Psychology at the University of South Carolina. He holds clinical membership and approved supervisory status in the American Association for Marriage and Family Therapy (AAMFT). You can reach Joshua at jgold@gwm.sc.edu.

9

The Boy Who Wouldn't Leave Home

Larry B. Golden

This family intervention with a young man suffering from schizophrenia extends over 15 years and 250 sessions. The expected — and respected — therapeutic goal of assisting a teenager in leaving home is thwarted by his disability and subsequent dependency. While most families find meaning in raising and launching children, this family does so by being mutually supportive. Golden must settle for stress management and small behavioral changes. He describes his approach as Kindly Old Uncle (or Aunt) Therapy.

Eighteen-year-old Melvin Frankl was referred for psychotherapy when he got in trouble chasing women through the aisles at a discount shopping store. One of his victims took offense and clobbered Melvin over the head with a tennis racket. When his father, Jacob, arrived on the scene, Melvin was still sitting on the floor rubbing the top of his head. The manager said that he would call the police if he saw Melvin in the store again. Jacob decided it was time to get his son into therapy.

Jacob Frankl was a career military officer who had been forced into early retirement by a "nervous breakdown." He maintained that the breakdown was intentionally caused by harassment from higher-ups. Jacob also believed an anesthetic accident during a tonsillectomy left Melvin with brain damage at age 3.

Lacey, Jacob's first wife and Melvin's mother, died in a car crash when Melvin was 11. Jacob was in no condition to care for Melvin and arranged for him to live with his (Jacob's) sister, Phyllis, and her alcoholic husband, Freddy, who verbally abused Melvin. This went on for 3 years until Jacob was able to resume his parental responsibilities.

Melvin was 14 when Jacob married Margot, a customer-service representative who handled complaints with the telephone company. Margot suffered from high blood pressure, diabetes, and migraines. Now in her early 60s and medically retired, her health problems had become life threatening.

I've maintained a private practice in psychology since 1976 with a specialization in marriage and family therapy. When I started with the Frankl family in 1984, their insurance paid 80 percent of my fee with unlimited sessions per year. Then a managed care company took over and required a $10.00 patient co-payment, a reduction in my fee, and a limit of 30 sessions per year. The managed care company has gone through several mergers with subsequent changes in policy, none for the better. In fairness, I haven't had any problems with them.

Melvin and his parents have signed a release for this publication. They were happy to do so, hoping that the telling of their story would help others. Of course, names and identifying information have been changed.

Conceptualization

When I realized how seriously disturbed Melvin was (this did not take very long), I insisted on a referral to a psychiatrist. I needed someone with the authority to medicate and hospitalize. Subsequently, I deferred to the psychiatrist's diagnosis of paranoid schizophrenia. Melvin had delusions and "word salad" speech. These symptoms manifested when Melvin was pushed beyond his very low stress threshold. He was simply unable to withstand the rigors of normal living.

On the Wechsler Intelligence Scale (WISC-R), Melvin's Verbal IQ was 84, his Performance IQ was 75, and his Full Scale IQ was 78. These scores placed Melvin at the borderline level of intellectual functioning. My opinion was that Melvin had a severe learning disability.

Melvin's affect was spongelike, in that he relied on others to tell him what he must be feeling. Rogers's reflective techniques backfired. Reflection of Melvin's feelings functioned as suggestions or even directions.

Therapist: It sounds to me as if you might be angry.
Melvin: I am getting very angry! (paces around, punches the wall)
Therapist: Calm down. I can't afford to repaint my walls. (Melvin sits down, apparently calm.)

From a systemic point of view, the Frankl family was enmeshed like peas in a pod. None of the three family members had a life outside the home. Jacob was medically retired and puttered around the house, Margot was heading in the same direction as fast as her myriad diseases could carry her (and eventually did), and Melvin hadn't a clue about leaving home.

My overall therapeutic goal for Melvin, as with any adolescent, was to support autonomous functioning. Subgoals were the following:

1. *Enhance the family's ability to cope with stressful situations.* When he wasn't stressed, Melvin's delusions eased up.

2. *Improve Melvin's social skills.* His odd speech and the bizarre content of his thoughts were obstacles to forming relationships. Hygiene also needed attention.

My strategies to achieve these goals were the following:

1. *Family therapy.* I intended to inspire the family to support Melvin's normal desires to leave home, to be employed, and, ultimately, to have a wife and family.

2. *Behavior modification.* I planned to enhance social skills using behavior modification because it works well with low-functioning individuals.

3. *Psychopharmacology.* By way of referral, I encouraged a medical intervention that could reduce Melvin's symptoms.

Process

I've seen the Frankl family for 250 sessions. As I read over my notes, I see enduring themes that surfaced in the first few visits. I'll explore these initial themes in detail and then note the highlights of subsequent years.

1984, Age 18. In the first session a three-ring circus format emerged that has endured over the years. At Jacob's request, I began the initial visit with "parent time" for him and Margot. Then I saw Melvin individually. I also reserved time for all three conjointly. During the parent portion, Jacob complained about the family's precarious financial position, which he saw as a consequence of his mistreatment at the hands of the U.S. military. Jacob was fearful that the military, in cahoots with other federal agencies, was plotting to renege on his benefits. He believed that the FBI was searching his garbage for evidence (of what?).

Margot had hoped to salvage her damaged stepson but, like so many stepparents, she underestimated the job. She attributed marital discord to Melvin-generated stress: "Our marriage is the *Titanic;* Melvin is the iceberg." She despaired that Melvin would never leave home. Of course, these beliefs generated rage. Jacob assumed the peacemaker role, trying to convince Margot that Melvin really wasn't so bad on the one hand, and coaching Melvin to watch his step with Margot on the other. This strategy didn't work. Margot was unappeased, and Melvin was noncompliant. When I caught them doing this dance and exposed it, the family took a "there we go again" attitude, more rueful than rageful.

Jacob told me about his hopes for what I could do for Melvin: He wanted a normal life for his son.

Then it was Melvin's turn. He was tall and lean, left-handed, and had nerdish glasses, chewed fingernails, and a bad stutter. Without shaking hands or offering a word of introduction, Melvin informed me that he was a high school junior at Christian Faith Academy, where he had found Jesus. Melvin complained that Jacob accused him of making long-distance calls to lawn mower companies: "God's judgment will be on him."

Melvin rambled obsessively about lawn mowers. He filled every conversational space with nonsense factoids, clichés, and redundancies.

Melvin:	The 20 horsepower John Deere riding mower would mow our lawn at 1066 Placer Court in 11 minutes and 42 seconds or 9 minutes and 52 seconds at full throttle as a matter of fact and Mr. Sears and Mr. Roebuck's 20 horsepower top-of-the-line riding mower has an automatic clutch for gosh sakes and could mow our typical normal average-size lawn at 1066 Placer Court in 9 minutes and 27 seconds for Pete's sake if only Mr. Jacob Frankl and Mrs. Margot Frankl the great poobahs would purchase or buy or make an investment in Mr. Sears and Mr. Roebuck's 20 horsepower, top-of-the-line riding mower for gosh sakes maybe once in a blue moon our grass would be cut within $2\frac{1}{2}$ and $2\frac{3}{4}$ inches in length that is recommended for ideal lawn care and our snotty neighbors for once wouldn't look down their snotty noses at the God-forsaken Frankl family for God's sake.
Therapist:	Do you like mowing the lawn?
Melvin:	Just call me the slave and the beast of burden and the indentured servant. If Mr. Jacob Frankl weren't so cheap and strapped for money and bankrupt and broke and unable to raise funds for gosh sakes and would purchase with a Master Card or American Express Card or Visa Card or Discover Card or simply write a check or pay with cash-in-hand or buy on credit a John Deere or a Sears and Roebuck top-of-the-line . . .

I had never had a conversation like this. Many years later, in 1997, I saw the movie *Shine*, about David Helfgott, a mentally ill musical genius who communicated with pressurized speech. David sounded like my client, Melvin! Except my Melvin was not a world-class pianist.

Therapist: What do you want to get from counseling?

Melvin: I simply want a high school diploma as a matter of fact because you can't get to first base or even third base without it for Pete's sake and I want to get married and I want to go to college and I want the pursuit of happiness for heaven's sake that every American male and female is entitled to in this life in these United States.

These were ambitious therapeutic goals. I invited Jacob and Margot back in, and they agreed to follow through on a referral to a psychiatrist.

At the second visit, I asked Melvin about the woman-chasing incident at the store. Melvin told me that he felt compelled to follow any female wearing red clothing. He admitted to stealing a girl's red purse at school because he "lusted after the color red." Of course, school authorities caught him. He hadn't taken anything out of the purse.

He wanted to describe his masturbatory fantasies, but I declined to hear them. He assured me that he would never do anything violent to any woman. I directed Melvin to look at his shoes when he felt a compulsion to stare at girls in red. This absurd directive actually helped.

Melvin acknowledged suicidal thoughts but denied any self-destructive plans.

In subsequent sessions during 1984, Melvin responded positively to my directions. I saw no evidence of teen rebellion. He behaved more like an eager-to-please 10-year-old. Margot wanted Melvin to shampoo his hair and dress appropriately. We put rewards in place for good grooming and got positive results.

Melvin reported that he relieved uncontrollable urges by throwing stones at Jacob's dog. I suggested that he throw rocks at the fence, instead. The next week he told me that he had substituted yelling at Jacob's dog for throwing stones. This wasn't a perfect solution, but Jacob's dog would probably agree that, "Sticks and stones will break my bones, but names will never hurt me."

I called Sandy Garza, Melvin's favorite teacher at Christian Faith Academy. She reported that Melvin is several years below grade level in academic achievement. "He's the most disturbed young man I've ever met. Some students feel threatened by him. Melvin told a girl, 'I know where you live.'" Ms. Garza reported that Melvin raised a chair over his head and threatened to throw it at several boys who were teasing him. Garza, herself, feels safe with him. She likes Melvin: "He's beautiful in prayer."

Melvin reported a poor response to antipsychotic medication. He was a little calmer and there was less nervous fingernail chewing, but the meds made him "dozy and headachy." Jacob "prescribed" a half dose. I pushed for a follow-up visit to the psychiatrist to fine tune the dosage or try something else. The psychiatrist cut the dosage in half and began stepping up gradually. Nothing doing! Jacob put Melvin's meds "on reserve" for emergencies. Melvin told me he will take his meds when he needs to make a good impression. (When will that be?) He's picked up on Jacob's distrust of the medical establishment. We've never found a psychiatrist whom Jacob trusted or a medication that was satisfactory. Sure enough, the sleepiness subsided when Melvin stopped taking his medication. Let's face it, medicine is a hit-or-miss affair.

1985, age 19. Melvin graduated with a bogus "vocational" diploma from Christian Faith Academy.

Margot and Jacob asked me about Melvin's driving, and I advised against it, imagining Melvin pursuing red cars at high speed. Melvin got his license anyway after failing the driving test several times. As it turns out, Melvin has never had a serious accident or even received a ticket (I would have heard about it). As age and disability overtake his parents, it's a good thing that Melvin can drive.

The Frankl family made their annual pilgrimage to Bremerton, Jacob's ancestral home, a rust-belt town in the Northeast. They usually did this during the winter and always had a miserable time.

Jacob's parents and his sister's family still lived there—the same sister whose husband Freddy had abused Melvin for three years after Lacey's death. Alcoholism had left Freddy in a crippled state, but Melvin was still afraid. I helped Melvin see that he was no longer a helpless child. We worked up a calming vision for Melvin to carry with him wherever he might go, an image of God holding his mother.

1986, age 20. Jacob finagled Melvin into Alta Vista Community College. I encouraged Melvin to take the bus to Alta Vista and check out a book at the library by way of preparation.

In January, Jacob brought a cake to celebrate that Melvin had passed the first semester at Alta Vista College, sort of. His grades were: "C," "IP" (In Progress), and "WP" (Withdrawn Passing). More impressive, he's ridden the bus daily.

Jacob tried without success to convince a professor to change Melvin's "IP" to a "C." During the second term, Melvin failed math and had to sit out a semester.

Melvin told me that he fears that he is gay. Jacob took him to a sex therapist, who debunked Melvin's belief that masturbation causes homosexuality.

It was obvious to me that Melvin wasn't college material, and I talked to Jacob about the Texas Rehabilitation Commission's assessment and training programs. Jacob didn't want Melvin working alongside "retards."

1987, age 21. Melvin arrived in my office with his arm in a cast. He had been hit by a car while riding his bike. According to a witness, Melvin had ignored a red light, and the police charged Melvin with the accident. Melvin complained of numbness of foot, flashbacks, nightmares, drowsiness, and loss of appetite. Jacob was looking for a lawyer because he wanted to sue the driver. He believed that the witness had been paid off by the insurance company. He asked me to write a letter stating that Melvin had suffered psychological distress as a consequence of the accident. I declined as I always do when asked to participate in legal battles. How can I be a therapist if I'm anxious about providing testimony?

Melvin was overwhelmed with anxiety about having to go to court. He lost 20 pounds and dropped all three courses at Alta Vista College. I counseled Melvin to stop obsessing about the trial and let his lawyer earn his keep. I prepared the family for hospitalization. What a bind for Melvin. He had to act crazier than he already was to win compensation in a lawsuit. The case came to nothing.

In a salvage effort, I called Alta Vista College's counseling center and greased the wheels for Melvin to get tutoring. Alfy, a very intense guy, took on Melvin as a holy crusade. Then he blamed Melvin for not trying hard enough to become transformed. I advised Alfy to limit his intervention to tutoring.

Alfy's angry outbursts had recalled Freddy's abuse, and Melvin confronted his father for failing to protect him. Jacob sincerely apologized, but Melvin wouldn't forgive.

1988, age 22. Melvin banged up the old Caddy, and Jacob covered for him with Margot: "Somebody did it while we were in the supermarket." Margot wasn't fooled. Melvin complains that he lost a mother's unconditional love and gained a step-mother's everlasting criticism.

1989, age 23. Margot complains of Melvin's obsessive hoarding: ". . . a pack rat just like his dad."

I was impressed when Melvin empathized with Margot's irritation with her employer.

Melvin:　　　　Margot works for a company that doesn't love her.

1990, age 24. I began a campaign to correct Melvin's perseveration and word salad. My strategy was to (1) cue him to slow down his speech; and (2) ask questions that required manifest versus automatic thought processing.

Melvin:　　　　(pressurized, rapid-fire speech) Melvin is up to his neck in trouble
　　　　　　　　and danger and evil and disaster and corruption and he may never
　　　　　　　　see the end or finish or finishing up or ending up for Pete's sake. . . .
Therapist:　　　Hold on, Melvin. Talk slowly. Use the first person, "I," instead of
　　　　　　　　speaking of yourself as if you were someone else, okay?
Melvin:　　　　Okay.
Therapist:　　　Tell me what kind of trouble you are in.

I have success with this intervention, but it doesn't seem to generalize.

1991, age 25. Where can Melvin spend time with other people and thereby practice social skills? Years ago he visited a church on his own. Based on a short conversation, the minister called Jacob and advised immediate institutionalization. So where can this strange young man be accepted?

The family was in good spirits while reminiscing about Christmases past, a reminder to me that not everything in their lives has been hurtful; mental health professionals get an earful of the depressing side of family life.

Melvin qualified for Social Security insurance because he was too disabled to function independently. I had written a letter to verify this. Was I slipping into a somnolent state, accepting Melvin's dependency, and giving up the good fight?

1992, age 26. Margot's diabetic symptoms have resulted in permanent retire-ment with a loss of income, depression for her, and increased stress for the Frankl family. I advised Melvin to be a pillar of strength for his parents in their hour of need. Clichés work with this guy.

1993, age 27. Melvin bounced some checks. He will repay Margot, and Jacob will teach him to balance his checkbook. What is Melvin buying? Most of the checks were made out to a local adult bookstore. Jacob feared that drugs could be on Melvin's shopping list and took Melvin's checkbook away. Now Melvin can only write checks under parental supervision.

His parents reported that Melvin punched the walls, saying, "If I went to Jesus, how would you and Margot deal with it?" Melvin was in teen rebellion at 27 years of age.

Margot and Jacob were struggling with the reality that Melvin would not be leav-ing home. We brainstormed how they could have a life apart despite his dependency. He could buy his own groceries and fix his own meals. He could live in his own cot-tage on the property. However, none of these things happened.

1994, 10 sessions, age 28. Thanks to Jacob's behind-the-scenes efforts, Melvin began volunteering three days per week at the San Antonio Bird Sanctuary, a bicycle ride from the Frankl home. Melvin's job was to maintain the outdoor public exhibit area. That meant picking up trash, cleaning the bathrooms, and watering plants. Melvin was proud of his job as "grounds engineer."

Managed care gets a lot of bad press, but I had a positive experience during my telephone request for additional sessions. The case manager suggested that Melvin should not go to Bremerton this year and thereby avoid the trauma of encountering his abusive uncle. This was "avoidable stress." It made perfect sense to me, and I dis-cussed it with the Frankl family. Melvin liked this idea because he was fearful of losing his job if he left town for two weeks. A coworker had been recently fired (Are volun-teers fired?); could the grounds engineer be next? For Jacob and Margot, it meant some time away although not exactly a honeymoon. So Melvin stayed home alone. During this time, I visited Melvin at the bird sanctuary. Jacob and Margot came home from two weeks in Bremerton to find Melvin and the house in good shape. Triumph!

1995, 15 sessions, age 29. Margot's diabetes was worse. Melvin told me that he absorbs the "grinding of family relationships." He described his father as a "paranoidal Casper Milquetoast."

1996, 2 sessions, age 30. The family met with my designated backup, Madeleine, during my vacation. She pushed autonomy. Would the Frankls want to try Madeleine for a change? They declined.

A colleague (con artist) at the bird sanctuary borrowed $100 from Melvin and then disappeared.

1997, 16 sessions, age 31. Melvin admired the slain star Selena. He recalled his mother, Lacey, as a "Marilyn Monroeish wallflower."

Melvin told me of daydreams of a normal life with a wife and children of his own. The irony is that he's become a family man, a mensch, in response to his parents' declining physical and mental capacity.

1998, 16 sessions, age 32. Melvin's Christmas wish was to hear loving words from Margot.

In order to not disturb Margot, Melvin asked Jacob what size plastic bowl he should use to store some leftovers, but Margot was angry. The kitchen was her domain, and she was boss of the bowls. The next time there was a kitchen question, Melvin went directly to Margot, and she softened her tough position.

What did Margot want for her birthday present? The menfolk should bake her a cake. Margot taught Melvin to bake a cake so he'd be ready for her birthday.

Jacob asked me to help him prepare Melvin for his and Margot's demise.

Therapist:	Jacob, what wisdom do you wish to pass down to your son?
Jacob:	Melvin, over my life I've had people do me dirt, but I want you to remember that revenge isn't the way.
Therapist:	Jacob, what are your concerns for Melvin after you and Margot die?
Jacob:	That he won't be able to take care of himself.
Therapist:	Melvin, where will you live after they pass away?
Melvin:	I could live in a group home. Maybe I'll find someone to marry.

1999, 5 sessions and ongoing, age 33. The family is adjusting to health crises that have become chronic. Parental anxiety regarding Melvin's involvement with the outside world is unabated.

Outcome

I saw this family for 250 sessions over 15 years. I deserve credit more for my patience and nurturance than for bringing about real change. My efforts to refer to specialists, especially psychiatrists, who might have attempted a medical approach, came to nothing.

I used behavior modification to reduce Melvin's word salad and make improvements in personal hygiene. I helped the Frankl family handle stress and thereby avoid any dangerous crises. Melvin has never been hospitalized or charged with a crime while under my care.

Like Jacob and Margot, I am worried about what will happen to Melvin when his parents die. This is the dread for any parents of a seriously disabled child. Besides putting away money in some sort of trust fund, I suppose that all these parents can do is hope that their beloved child will rise to the challenge and pray that the world will be compassionate. Perhaps Melvin will find work. Maybe he'll team up with another individual or live in a halfway house. In the meantime, Melvin has a place at the Frankl table. Since becoming a department chair at UTSA, I no longer have time for a private practice, and so I've referred the Frankl family to another therapist.

■ Discussion

Progress in this case offends my beliefs about family therapy. I thought that I was supposed to help children achieve independence. At the child's 13th birthday, the traditional coming of age, Jewish parents praise God: "Blessed be He who has freed me from the chastisement of this child." Even if they were Jewish, Jacob and Margot will never utter such a prayer of thanksgiving. Melvin is disabled and he can't manage his own money. His parents are in poor health and depend on Melvin's physical strength. Under these circumstances, autonomy isn't a realistic goal. In such cases, a strong sense of familial obligation deserves my respect as a functional adaptation.

What should I label this so-called therapy I've conducted with the Frankl family? I joined the family system (I hope I didn't merely collude), and I offered consistent support that kept the stress at a manageable level. I honored these parents for bearing up under the burden of caring for a disabled child. I counseled patience. I praised Melvin for looking after his parents in their dotage. I set appropriate boundaries, declining Jacob's attempts to enlist me in his paranoid adventures.

I think I'll call this *Kindly Old Uncle/Aunt Therapy* (KOU/AT)! Will Goldenian KOU/AT take its rightful place beside person-centered, cognitive, psychodynamic, and existential approaches? Maybe not. KOU/AT doesn't exactly roll off the tongue.

Biographical Statement

Larry B. Golden, Ph.D., is chair of the Department of Counseling, Educational Psychology, and Adult & Higher Education at the University of Texas at San Antonio. He is a licensed psychologist and specializes in counseling with couples and families. Larry has published several books, including *Helping Families Help Children: Family Interventions with School-Related Problems, Preventing Adolescent Suicide, The Ethical Standards Casebook, 4th edition,* and *Case Studies in Child and Adolescent Counseling, 3rd edition.* You can reach Larry at lgolden@utsa.edu.

10

Coming Out

Bibiana M. Gutierrez

Alexandra was a 38-year-old mother and wife who came out as a lesbian in a heterosexual marriage. While this was an individual client, there were striking and inescapable systemic implications. Gutierrez concedes, "I intellectually understood and was aware of the concept of a mixed orientation marriage but had not yet experienced this first hand." Gutierrez is well-grounded in psychodynamic, systems, and multicultural theories. But how useful are theories in understanding a case like this? My opinion is that Gutierrez' "strategy" is best described as a therapeutic journey.

Alexandra was a 38-year-old mother, wife, and student who came out as a lesbian in a heterosexual marriage a year earlier. She was depressed and anxious. Her first counselor at our university counseling center had left to take another job. It was important to Alexandra that I would be able to continue counseling her in my private practice if she exhausted the 12-session limit. We agreed to work within the short-term guidelines of the counseling center with the understanding that she would transition into longer-term therapy with me or another provider outside of the university counseling center. The center at that time allowed clients to continue therapy with the same therapist in private practice, if the client so chose.

It was clear that, although I would be working with Alexandra as an individual, others would be impacted. Over the course of her therapy, Alexandra's identity, family, spouse and children, social support system, and career path would ultimately be affected. I think that this wasn't fully apparent to either of us when we first began this journey.

Conceptualization

During the course of my training and experience, I have come to be known as someone with some expertise in working with gay, lesbian, bisexual, and transgendered clients. This reputation, I believe, occurred through my targeted outreach with gay, lesbian, bisexual, and transgendered student organizations. Eventually, through word-of-mouth, over half of my caseload consisted of this population.

I intellectually understood and was aware of the concept of a mixed orientation marriage (one partner in a marriage coming out as a gay, lesbian, or bisexual person), but had not yet experienced this firsthand in the course of my work. Although I felt I had enough theoretical grounding to help guide me, it was quickly apparent to me that this case was new and different. I was still confident in my ability to provide a safe and trusting therapeutic relationship that I believe is critical for clients to be able to explore such core identity issues.

I usually work from a psychodynamic perspective but use interventions from other theoretical orientations, especially in short-term therapy. Although I used a psychodynamic theory to understand Alexandra's worldview, relationships with others, ways of coping, and vulnerabilities to depression and anxiety, I felt it was not particularly useful in understanding her presenting issues. I found it more productive to use a narrative approach while being mindful of developmental, multicultural, relational, and systemic theories. I had solid theory to help ground me as a therapist, but I was both unsure and excited about where the process would take us.

▪ Process

Early Sessions (1999) Alexandra dealt with immediate issues related to her coming out. She talked about the ripple effects of coming out on others in her life. She was anxious about her marriage and her family.

An early challenge was managing my heterosexist biases about monogamy; my assumption was that the healthiest configuration is a monogamous, heterosexual marriage. Alexandra and her spouse, Ramsey, came to a mutual decision to have an "open marriage" as she began exploring her newly discovered sexuality. They agreed to continue in the marriage with the option of seeing other people. The purpose of this decision was to give Alexandra an opportunity to fully explore her sexual identity so as to make an informed decision about whether or not to continue in the marriage. Through a conscious effort to maintain an open mind, I felt able to accept the possibility that this open marriage could be functional.

I encouraged Alexandra to get emotional support. It was fortunate that Ramsey was able to be accepting and supportive of her coming out. Of course, this is not always the case in these types of situations. For some couples this process is colored by resentment, blame, guilt, and even rage on the part of the straight spouse. Even though Ramsey was her primary source of support, Alexandra needed support from others because much of her distress dealt with whether or not the marriage would survive. She came to understand that it was not helpful for her or her spouse to process *all* of their feelings with each other. Ramsey, at this point in time, wanted to continue in the marriage if she so desired. A great deal of Alexandra's therapy in this beginning stage focused on her decision about whether or not to stay in the marriage. And if she were to stay, how they would work it out.

As I was able to help Alexandra freely explore her emotions, she began to access positive feelings and experiences associated with becoming more true to herself. The anxiety and depression subsided, although a subclinical level of anxiety remained and was easily triggered by unexpected crises. In fact, anxiety was a part of Alexandra's emotional life prior to coming out. At times her anxiety soared and led to deep depression. In the beginning stages of her therapy, Alexandra experienced a chronic state of imbalance and distress.

I encouraged Alexandra to learn to manage her thoughts, behaviors, and responses to stress. When anxiety or depression got out of hand, I referred her to be evaluated for medication. The medication helped, but after awhile she got better at managing her symptoms and no longer needed medication.

Living in a fairly conservative area of the United States, Alexandra felt isolated. She did not feel welcomed by the lesbian community when she attempted to connect with them. She experienced pressure to reject her marriage in order to be fully accepted. She then discovered chat rooms and list serves on the internet, a source of support that had been created by and for gay men, lesbians, bisexuals and their heterosexual partners from around the world.

After some time, Alexandra realized the limitations of this "virtual support" and felt ready to take the next step. This was a time of great expectations and anxiety in her therapy, as she prepared to meet her "virtual support" in person in a large city out of state. I helped her get ready. We talked about the possibility of her first same-sex sexual encounter, her spouse's reactions, and how to explain her trip to her children since she was not yet "out" to them. Alexandra stated that she felt like a teenager again with a teenager's hopes, desires, anxieties, and fears.

This trip started off a whole series of adolescent-like crushes and disappointments. Alexandra and Ramsey began negotiating the rules of their open marriage. During this early stage, Alexandra's spouse began a relationship, including a sexual encounter with his best woman friend. This released a cascade of feelings for Alexandra that brought her closer to difficult conclusions about her ability to continue in the marriage.

Middle Sessions (2000–2001) The sessions at the university counseling center were used up. It was ethically important for me to inform Alexandra of all options, including community agencies. She decided to continue with me in my private practice.

There were several incidents that told me that Alexandra was ready to take a more candid look at her family, her children, her parents, and her new love relationship. The ripples of the stone that had been thrown a year and a half ago were moving further out. This was a time fraught with periods of great anxiety and depression. We often spoke of the "storms and hurricanes" in her life as occurring so frequently that she rarely felt a moment of stability.

Probably one of the most significant events in Alexandra's life was entering her first love relationship with another woman, Debbie. Feelings of increased comfort and pride emerged as Alexandra approached the two-year anniversary of her coming out as a lesbian.

It became clear to Alexandra that she probably did not want to continue in her marriage, but this realization was so frightening that it occurred gradually over the course of a year. It was painful to Alexandra to think of ending her marriage to the person with whom she had planned to grow old, who was the father of her children and her best friend.

My role as therapist seemed to expand beyond the traditional boundaries. Debbie was going through a parallel process of coming out as a lesbian in her own marriage that included children. I had to balance supporting Alexandra as an individual, while being attentive to the significant others in her life. It was as if I was conducting family therapy with most of the members in absentia. It was important to me to acknowledge Ramsey's grieving and depression and how this might affect their long-term co-parenting relationship. Debbie was becoming Alexandra's primary relationship.

Alexandra and Ramsey decided that she should come out to the children. I saw it as my role to prepare her for a range of reactions and outcomes. I wanted her to think carefully about what she would say. The ripples were spreading. Coming out to her parents was a fearful thing, but the fear made it very clear why it had taken so long to discover her true sexual identity. Their strong antigay religious beliefs would make it all the harder for them to accept her. Alexandra went to her high school reunion and her first gay pride event accompanied by Debbie. She seemed to be entering a more stable period in her life.

I recommended that Alexandra consider joining a Gay, Lesbian, and Bisexual Support Group that I was running. I had mentioned it to her earlier in her treatment, but at that time she wasn't ready. The group seemed a perfect venue for her to take a risk in a protected, controlled setting. I knew from experience the healing power of a group setting, yet I was hopeful but unsure about the group's willingness to accept her.

Overall, the group experience helped Alexandra. She felt accepted even though she was married. She also benefited from the opportunity she had to help others who were at earlier stages of their coming out. The group offered her support for applying to graduate school to pursue a new career direction.

__Later Sessions (2002)__ Alexandra worried about what colleagues at work and in graduate school would think if they knew that she was a lesbian. For the sake of their children, Alexandra and Ramsey decided to delay the divorce until the children were older. Financial issues were more easily and amicably managed if they stayed legally married. But they had decided to separate households due to Ramsey's job. When Ramsey developed a new love relationship, I helped Alexandra navigate the multiple family systems in a manner that was most beneficial for her and her children.

This was an exciting, busy, and anxiety-provoking time, as Alexandra balanced being a single parent, going to college, working part-time, and applying for graduate school. There was the possibility of moving out of state to go to graduate school. What would this mean for her children? What was Debbie's plan for her own marriage, children, and career?

Outcome

I think Alexandra made a great deal of progress over the course of the three years she was in therapy with me. She addressed the identity, couple, family, and career issues related to her coming out as a lesbian. She became more self-accepting, comfortable, and confident. She learned to manage anxiety and depression. She pursued her dream career. I think I was able to offer a place for her to process, celebrate, grieve, and receive encouragement during the course of her journey. On the eve of termination, Alexandra reported that she felt she was still "toddling," as toddlers do when they learn to walk, but definitely felt more grounded in her new sense of self.

Discussion

If I had met Alexandra as a neophyte therapist, I don't think I would have been ready to go on this journey. Even as a seasoned therapist, I did not know where the journey would take us, but at least I could tolerate my own anxiety and ambiguity. This experience made multicultural counseling more real for me. In order to provide a safe environment, I had to become aware of and address my personal biases. I read the research about counseling with lesbians, and I consulted with colleagues. I could not have helped Alexandra address her own heterosexist biases and homophobic fears if I had not yet done so for myself. I may have done her harm.

I was deeply touched and felt it was a gift from Alexandra that she gave me permission to share her experience with others. It was her wish as well as mine that other clients and therapists would benefit from our journey.

Biographical Statement

Bibiana M. Gutierrez, Ph.D., is an assistant professor at the University of Texas at San Antonio in the Department of Counseling, Educational Psychology, and Adult & Higher Education. She is a licensed psychologist and has maintained a private practice since 1999. Bibiana completed her doctorate in Counseling Psychology from Texas A & M University in 1996. Her clinical experiences have included working with adults, adolescents, children, families, and groups in inpatient and outpatient settings. She has conducted research and presented in the areas of multicultural competency, homophobia, and domestic violence. Bibiana's growing areas of interest include gay, lesbian, bisexual, and transgendered issues, multicultural and gender issues, psychoneuroimmunobiology, and social activism. You can reach Bibiana at bgutierrez@utsa.edu.

11

Holding the Family Together

Fred J. Hanna

Fred Hanna is charged with treating 2-year-old Joshua's constipation. Hanna immediately picks up on marital conflict as a contributing factor. Much to his frustration, the couple adamantly declines his invitation to work on their relationship. This case, both in its obvious success and subtle limitations, illustrates the power of a family-systems perspective. Hanna makes good use of strategic techniques such as reframing and paradox.

When a mother called our small private practice and told me she was having a problem with her 2-year-old child, I knew exactly what to do. I had no experience with a child that young, so I told her that I would not be a good choice as a therapist. The woman would not be denied. "You helped a friend of ours with a teenage daughter," she asserted, "and she highly recommended you, and we really need some help."

"I am sorry," I said, "but you are asking me to help you with a situation that I do not feel competent to deal with. I have ample experience with adolescents but little with children under 12 and none whatsoever with 2-year-olds. I strongly suggest that you see a professional who specializes in very young children."

"But we've already done that. We've been to a child psychiatrist and a child psychologist. Joshua hasn't had regular bowel movements for six months. His last movement was nearly two weeks ago. Our family doctor says that this is a serious problem. She pleaded, "Won't you at least see us one time and then decide if you can help? We have excellent insurance coverage."

I explained that bowel movements could be added to the list of problems for which I had no professional training. I asked her what she learned from the psychiatrist and family physician about Josh's physiological condition. She told me that Josh checked out all right physically. Both the psychiatrist and the psychologist wondered if Josh was under any unusual stress. I asked if her husband was willing to attend the sessions and was assured that he was very willing.

"Okay," I said hesitantly, hardly believing that I was agreeing. I found myself admiring the woman's persuasive ability. "We'll try one session to discuss the possibility of whether I can be of help."

Conceptualization

Based on the initial visit, I'll set the scene. Nick and Donna were in their early 30s and lived in Chicago. They were attractive, well dressed, and exuded an air of prosperity. Donna was tall and trim with moderately long, bright red hair and a few freckles. Nick was dark, a touch overweight, and well over 6 feet tall. While both had been born in the United States, her cultural background was Scandinavian and his was Italian. Both were sharp, successful lawyers. Nick specialized in civil cases, and Donna's practice was in worker's compensation. They had been married for six years, and Josh was their only child. Donna had been married twice previously and had no children from either of those marriages. Nick was the noncustodial parent of three children by a previous marriage.

Joshua seemed a pleasant, lovable little boy. He was light skinned with brown hair and brown eyes and was very quiet. He looked normal and healthy, although his eyes revealed either preoccupation or distance. He seemed sad to me, although he readily smiled when Nick joked with him. Nick and Donna assured me that Josh had suffered from virtually no medical problems prior to constipation. They reiterated that Josh was going for 10 days to two weeks at a time without a bowel movement and that the problem had persisted for nearly six months. They were worried and mystified. I confessed that it was a mystery to me as well.

Most of this first session was tied up in details about Joshua's toilet habits and personality traits. In my ineptitude and lack of experience with young children, I tried talking with Josh directly. He declined to answer even simple questions. I asked him, "Are you happy?" and "Do you like to go potty?" The blank stares I received left me feeling quite helpless and not a little ridiculous.

Watching Nick and Donna shift uncomfortably when I asked Josh if he was happy was informative. I'm sure they were unaware of their nonverbal cues. The thought dawned on me right then that a systems approach was best. A considerable distance seemed to exist between Nick and Donna, as they seldom made eye contact with each other. I observed that they were not only distant but cold and subtly antagonistic, in spite of a strained attempt to put up a cordial front. Each seemed willing to blame the other for stress that Josh was experiencing, although neither identified what that stress might have been.

When I asked about previous counseling, they told me that, before Joshua was born, they had seen two therapists for marital problems. It "had not helped at all." I took this to mean that exploring the territory of their marriage would be unproductive.

I asked how their marriage was going. I wasn't quite ready for Donna's instant reply, "That really has nothing to do with Joshua." Nick also protested, "Oh no! Not that again." Donna was adamant that their relationship was not the issue. It was the vehemence of their protest that redoubled my interest in a systems approach.

Systems theory treats a family as interlocking parts or members that make up an interrelated whole. A change in one aspect of the system leads to change in the others. If the marital relationship changed, Josh's bowels might move!

Kurt Lewin said, "There is nothing so practical as a good theory." At this point, I had little else. I told Nick and Donna that I planned to approach Joshua's problem indirectly. I explained that even if it seemed embarrassing to them or otherwise uncomfortable, I needed information about their relationship. I said that I would not impose marital therapy per se and that my primary focus was on Joshua's problem. I suggested a maximum of eight sessions to explore this approach and they agreed.

I silently resolved to trust that systems theory and my therapeutic instincts would provide a therapeutic resolution for Joshua's constipation. I braced myself for failure.

According to the *DSM-IV-TR*, Josh could not be diagnosed with encopresis because he was younger than 4 and had not been passing feces into inappropriate places. On those rare occasions when Joshua did "poop," he always did so into a small "potty" or his diaper. After three sessions, I diagnosed him as meeting criteria for Adjustment Disorder with Anxiety due to Joshua's probable fears and insecurities arising from being placed in the middle of the fighting, threats of leaving, and general animosity between his parents. Parental fighting caused anxiety, which, in turn, caused constipation. That was before I saw the bigger picture.

■ Process

<u>Session 1.</u> The first session is detailed in the previous Conceptualization section.

<u>Session 2.</u> This session was a perfect example of what Carl Whitaker called the Battle for Initiative. A semblance of a working relationship took form when I challenged them to work with me for Joshua's benefit. I asked Nick and Donna to paint a verbal picture of Josh's home environment. Part of this painting required them to talk about their marriage. Both said that this sounded suspiciously like marital therapy, and that was not the reason they were employing me. They reiterated that attempts at marital therapy had been "a waste of time," although neither felt antagonism toward the therapists. Of course, I was curious about what had happened. They told me that the therapists "didn't know what they were doing."

They agreed to talk about their relationship after I asked pointedly, "What is more important, concealing the embarrassment of your relationship or using it to help Joshua get through this?" I needed to know about the emotional climate that Josh experienced at home.

By way of reassurance, I provided stark examples of families with serious dysfunction, such as physical abuse, sexual abuse, children of criminal parents, and families with defiant, drug-abusing teenagers. Their own problems were not so bad after all.

Therapist: You insisted on seeing me. At least give me the opportunity to work as best as I know how.

They reluctantly agreed to disclose the details, quality, and character of their relationship. I learned that their marriage lacked passion or interest. Both were unhappy with their sexual relationship, and each accused the other of not caring. They were quite matter-of-fact about it, but it was clear that plenty of hurt and anger simmered below the surface. I knew that eventually I would have a shot at doing marital counseling but first I had to, as family therapists like to say, "join the system." I was not hesitant to tell them that if they thought the eight-session commitment was a mistake, we would stop.

<u>Session 3.</u> Formality dissipated as we dropped the medical talk of constipation, bowel movements, and stools. Nick eventually started speaking directly: "The kid just refuses to shit," or "If I had that much shit in me, I would have burst by now." Donna would laugh uneasily at these comments. Her words were more genteel: "going potty" and "holding his poop." Thank God, they had a sense of humor.

They reported that communication alternated between days without speaking and in-your-face screaming. During the latter they used their obviously high intelligence and verbal skills to insult. Nick complained that Donna called him stupid, idiotic, arrogant, and selfish while holding Joshua on her lap. He had begged her not to hold the child when they fought because she was hurting him by doing so.

Donna informed me that Nick was not so likely to engage in name calling, although he sometimes called her ignorant. His style was disdain, a deliberate lack of warmth, prolonged bouts of the silent treatment, and both subtle and direct comments designed to make her feel like an incompetent mother. Both often made statements along the lines of "I don't need you," or "Get out of my house," or "I am outta here." They told me that they had given up on their relationship and agreed about a year ago that they would stay together "for the sake of the baby." I was getting a picture of what Joshua was experiencing.

Session 4. I asked Nick and Donna to describe the scene when they tried to get Josh to defecate: the parents excitedly encouraged Josh to poop, promising him all kinds of rewards (such as expensive toys). Generally, Josh had not responded.

Therapist:	Tell me if I'm wrong, but it seems to me that the only time Josh ever sees you happy and enthusiastic together is when you are trying to get him to poop. Is that accurate?
Nick:	That's probably true.
Donna:	That could be.
Therapist:	Is it also true that the only time he sees both of you working together and agreeing with each other is when you are trying to get him to poop?
Donna:	I hate to say it, but that's true too.

I was still not entirely sure where I was going, but I felt that inner surge of energy that tells me when I'm onto something, that a therapeutic door was opening!

Therapist:	What is Josh like when he is on the potty and you are encouraging him? Does he seem happy, sad? What?
Nick:	It's strange. It's kind of like he is happy, like he is enjoying all the attention. I have always wondered if his holding it in is just his way of trying to get attention. He spends a lot of time in day care, and we are not around as much as we should be.
Donna:	Yes. The psychologist said that Nick was probably right about not spending enough time. But we can't figure out how to deal with his attention seeking.
Therapist:	There are lots of ways to get attention. I wonder why Josh has chosen this method.

Now, at last, my wheels were turning. I was beginning to understand little Joshua. During the following week I had an insight that helped me formulate a plan for our next session.

Session 5. I began by saying that I had been thinking about Joshua all week. I summarized previous sessions and told them that I wanted to bounce an idea off them. They nodded, curious to see what I had come up with. I presented my reframe of Joshua's problem.

Therapist:	I think I may know what the problem is really about, and I don't think it is about seeking attention.

Nick:	What is it then?
Therapist:	(slowly and deliberately) Joshua is ... HOLDING ... the family together.
Nick and Donna:	(almost in unison) What?
Therapist:	By not pooping, Joshua is holding his family, your family, together. The only time he sees you happy and cooperating with each other is when you are trying to get him to poop. It is the only time that he feels as if he has a happy family. He believes that if he can continue to hold his poop, his effort can make both of you happy and stop your fighting. He may be inspired in his efforts due to his fear that you will be leaving him because of your various threats to each other. What do you think?"
Donna:	(turning to her husband) We're screwing him up!
Nick:	Do you really think that could be it?
Therapist:	I am convinced that Joshua is not a selfish attention seeker. He's a little hero trying to save his parents from their own hostility.

Nick and Donna were caught off guard. They took in my reframe with solemnity. The rest of the session was spent processing the implications.

Session 6. I asked if they had second thoughts about my hypothesis. Both said they had not, that it made sense, and that they had been talking about it all week. But what should they do? I explained Bowen's concept of triangulation. Then I braced myself. I told them that I was about to suggest an approach that they might not like. I proposed that they work on their relationship in therapy so that Joshua could experience a happy, loving, family environment.

Nick:	(loudly and immediately) Oh no! We agreed that we are NOT going to do any more marriage counseling.
Donna:	(adamantly shaking her head) You said that we would not have to do that.
Therapist:	Okay. Then you'll have to learn to fake it. Pretend you are getting along marvelously. Take Joshua out to McDonald's, the movies, the mall, the backyard, or anywhere. But go there together. And most important: act as if you're happy and enthusiastic. It's that attitude on your part that's important. Show him that he doesn't have to stage bathroom dramas in order to get you two to stay together.
Donna:	And we should not fight in front of him anymore, right?
Therapist:	Right. At all costs, avoid any further displays of antagonism, name calling, threats, and the silent treatment. I especially suggest that you should avoid all references of any kind to the effect that one or both of you are leaving, as this may be a source of great anxiety to Joshua. I am asking for a truce on behalf of your child.

Both nodded, looking grim. I asked them to shake hands on their truce. We discussed the details of the strategy for some time. At the end of the session, I said, "I would like for you to maintain the truce for two weeks. Give me a call next week, and let me know how it's going." I then set up an appointment to see them in two weeks.

Session 7. At the end of one week, Donna called to say they were carrying out their assignment, difficult as it was. Joshua had pooped that day! She sounded excited and hopeful.

When they came in for the next session, they reported that Joshua had pooped twice in the previous week. The session lasted only a half-hour. We talked about what they were doing to fake a good relationship and how Joshua was responding. I scheduled a session in two weeks but requested a call in a week to keep me informed.

Session 8. The phone call the following week was positive. Donna informed me that Josh had pooped three times that week.

When they arrived for the session the following week, they reported that Joshua was moving his bowels every other day, and his physician was pleased. Nick and Donna expressed gratitude. I then smiled and said to them, "Do you think that you should be working on your relationship?"

Nick chuckled and said, "Oh no, here we go!" While his tone was good humored, neither partner was ready to brave my challenge any time soon.

Outcome

I followed up with a telephone call after three months and got Nick and Donna on the phone at once. Nick informed me that Joshua was having regular bowel movements. Donna expressed relief that she hadn't even thought about Joshua's problem for quite a while.

A month later, Donna called and told me that she was referring a friend to me for therapy. Joshua was still doing well. I asked how she and Nick were getting along. She replied that they were doing "a little better."

"Are you still faking it?"

She laughed and said, "Yeah, I guess so."

Discussion

This case remains unique in my experience. It was a clean success from the viewpoint of the apparent resolution of the presenting problem. This was one of those rare outcomes that could be measured obviously in terms of number of bowel movements per week.

On the more ambiguous side, it is still surprising to me that Nick and Donna were not interested in working on the difficulties in their relationship. There is no question, however, that they clearly realized the effect their relationship had on their son.

In retrospect, I believe the key was the reframe of Joshua as a hero who was holding the family together in the only way he could. The suggestion to "fake" their getting along had much utility in a paradoxical fashion. It had the effect of motivating the couple to treat each other better.

This couple required a firm, direct approach. They were both remarkably intelligent and persuasive, although their strength did not lie in the psychological domain. Their effort to get me to see them as an "innocent" couple with a problem child was transparent.

Although I did not know how to reach him verbally, I empathized with Joshua immediately. My own parents had argued and yelled in the presence of their children. I believe I knew how Joshua was feeling when this happened in his family.

Nick and Donna's respect for me grew as I gently but firmly insisted that they tell me the truth about their relationship and exposed the detrimental effects on Joshua. I regret that they persisted in keeping me away from the problems in their marital relationship.

My guess is that this couple will eventually divorce unless they take the risk of getting into marriage counseling. Both Nick and Donna refused to confront any personal material that was anxiety producing, except when it was for the sake of their son.

In regard to my initial refusal to see this couple, this case taught me to always strive to be open to new challenges and not draw premature conclusions about whom I can help and whom I cannot. I saw clearly how 2-year-old Joshua played the role of the "family healer." Although I had worked with many families in the past and had used many family therapy techniques, this was the case that convinced me, once and for all, of the value, validity, and relevance of the family systems approach.

With the benefit of hindsight, I would not have done much of anything differently. I sure would like a shot at working on the marital relationship!

Biographical Statement

Fred Hanna, Ph.D., is a professor in the Department of Counseling and Human Services at Johns Hopkins University in Baltimore, Maryland. He presents workshops about difficult adolescents and consults with schools and community agencies. Fred is the author of a book, *Therapy with Difficult Clients: Using the Precursors Model to Awaken Change*. You can reach Fred via e-mail at fhanna@jhu.edu.

12

From Russia with Love

Karin B. Jordan

An American-born husband and a Russian-born wife move from Russia to the United States, and their relationship is in jeopardy. No neat diagnostic labels exist that describe the multilayered linguistic and cultural misunderstandings encountered by Seth and Katia. This couple was fortunate in finding their way to Karin Jordan. In addition to her solution-oriented approach, Jordan brought to bear her personal experience as an immigrant in a German-American marriage.

I am a member of a group practice of marriage and family therapists in a large eastern city. Seth, 36, American-born, and Katia, 35, Russian-born, asked for my help because they "couldn't stand it anymore." Seth and Katia's marriage had deteriorated ever since they had moved to the United States from Russia a few months earlier.

Katia was the identified patient because, according to Seth, she did not understand or want to understand "the American way." Seth had been told by a friend, one of my former clients, that I had emigrated to the United States from Germany as an adult and had successfully managed the challenge of acculturating to this country. Seth hoped I might be able to relate to Katia's experience. Previous counseling with an American-born male therapist had failed because Katia felt misunderstood.

Payment was in cash because marital therapy wasn't covered by their managed care plan. I saw the couple weekly for conjoint sessions for a total of eight sessions and one booster session $4\frac{1}{2}$ weeks post-termination.

■ Conceptualization

This couple struggled with divisive dissimilarities in belief systems, communication styles, and behaviors, which were rooted in cultural differences. While living in Russia, Seth and Katia had successfully handled transactions in certain situations, but the recent move to the United States had thrown them for a loop! Katia was perplexed that her Russian behaviors were no longer appropriate. Her American husband had resumed his "Americanness" and expected her to follow his lead.

Katia's feeling of being misunderstood by the previous therapist needed to be addressed. I worked hard to join with her. I think it helped that I was a female.

I chose the solution-oriented approach because I like its assumption that people do the best they can in a given situation. I value its respect for the client's circumstances and focus on observable phenomena. And, of course, it's relatively brief and economical.

Here are some examples of solution-oriented thinking. Seth and Katia were what solution-oriented counselors call "customers." Both partners were in counseling because they saw it as an opportunity to change. My first step was to find out what they perceived the problem to be and how each one of them experienced the severity of the problem. I used the *scaling question,* in which clients are asked to rate behaviors or feelings on a scale of 1 to 10 as a way to assess their growth throughout therapy. I like to use the solution-oriented Formula First Session Task (FFST) to find out what the client wants to hold onto and *not* change. As a homework assignment, I asked Katia and Seth to tell me if anything happened during the week that they wanted to see continue.

Since the overarching problem was the couple's cultural differences, treatment had to be designed to help the couple bridge these differences. The goal was to assist the couple to move from cultural conflict to a *transcultural* perspective. Each partner in this couple system was encouraged to accept and understand certain aspects of the other's belief system, communication style, and behavior. This meant that the couple needed to talk about these things both in and outside the counseling session through exercises in the session and homework assignments. I encouraged Katia and Seth to regard counseling as a process, something they could return to again and again as they felt the need.

Process

Session 1. Katia and Seth attended the first session and completed all initial paperwork (i.e., disclosure form). I delivered my standard introduction to solution-oriented therapy.

Therapist:	Our relationship is a partnership. I give you the best that I can as a clinician, and I expect your best effort in return. I cannot fix your problem, but I will help you find new solutions and rediscover old forgotten solutions as a way to solve your problem. I regard both of you as the experts on your life experiences. I will count on you to set me straight if I misinterpret anything you say.

Katia immediately asked about my struggles in acculturating.

Therapist:	You know, the first few months after I came to the U.S., everything was different and exciting, but then I became confused. Everything was so different.
Katia:	Yes. You mean how to behave and what to do?
Therapist:	Yes. Customs that I was raised with in Germany suddenly didn't fit. I was taught to address people formally as Mr. and Mrs., but in the U.S. everything is so casual.
Katia:	Yes. You understand what I mean! People here are on a first-name basis before they even know each other.
Therapist:	Seth, what are your hopes for therapy?
Seth:	My wife has difficulty adjusting to the American culture, and I am here to help her.
Katia:	I have difficulty with adjusting to all the change. You see, things are different here. Even Seth is so different. In Russia he was more respectful. He uses a lot of bad language now, especially with his friends.

My next step was to clarify if, and what, each spouse wanted to change. In solution-focused terms, I wanted to know if one or both were (1) *visitor,* who merely check counseling out; (2) *complainant,* who complain but don't want to work; or (3) *customers,* who want to do something about their problems. These clients both clearly indicated that they were committed to do whatever it took to make this relationship work. I had customers!

Therapist:	Please describe who is doing what, when, and where when the two of you are fighting.
Katia:	It generally happens when Seth's friends come over to watch a baseball game or barbecue. Seth tells me to wear jeans or shorts. We then start arguing. Seth will say, "Why can't you be more like an American woman?" I tell him, "You knew who I was when you married me." He then will use very bad language, you see, the "bitch" and the "F" word. His friends will do the same the whole afternoon. I don't understand. Why do they have to talk like this?
Seth:	(very fidgety) When I have friends over, she wants to dress up, and everyone else dresses down. She makes everyone uncomfortable. She gets upset when we drink beer and have a good time.

I learned that when they lived in Russia, the couple socialized with Katia's family. Her family was dressed formally (as compared to the United States), and profanity was unacceptable. When Seth lived in Russia, he did as the Russians did. He was glad to move back to the United States because he felt stifled in Russia. Because he was flexible and followed the Russians in Russia, why couldn't Katia follow the American way now? A power struggle had ensued.

Therapist:	You two are culturally bilingual. You "spoke Russian" together fluently when you were courting in Russia. When you moved to the United States, Katia kept "speaking Russian," the culture of your romance, while Seth reverted to his native language and culture. What culture and language do you want to speak and celebrate now? This is about language, culture, and values.

I wanted to normalize this process.

Therapist:	You know, this process is not much different from what other couples have to go through. We all bring our own heritage with us, our family of origin, the family we grew up in. Every couple seeks the right blend, the perfect mix, to agree on their own unique language. Does that make sense?

The couple understood my bilingual metaphor. I assigned the solution-focused Formula First Session Task: Between now and the next time we meet, I want you to watch closely so you can tell me what happens in your marriage that you want to continue to have happen.

Session 2. I asked how things had been going. Both partners smiled, looked at each other and then at me. Katia reported that they had been trying harder and that Seth's friends had spent less time with them. Seth was also happy with their efforts. I amplified this welcome change by asking the couple to turn their chairs to face each other. One partner was to talk about what he/she experienced as positive. The other partner was to listen and then restate, in his/her own words, what he/she heard. Katia affirmed that Seth had been more attentive and less critical of her dress code and had spent more time with her and less with his friends. Seth declared that Katia was trying harder to "fit in," was more accepting when Seth used strong language, and was more affectionate.

My next step was to help the couple move from "head to heart." I had each partner identify how he/she felt about the other's behavior last week. Katia and Seth easily identified their feelings and both reported that last week felt like "the good old days," when their relationship was filled with love and joy.

To continuously measure the change that each partner was experiencing, I introduced the scaling question, "How do you rate your marital problem on a scale of 1 to 10, with 10 indicating your problem is totally resolved?" Seth rated the problem as being a 4, up from a 2 the previous week, while Katia rated the problem a 3, improved from a 1.5. I asked the couple what they needed to do to achieve a 1-point gain during the coming week. The couple agreed that they should do more of the same kinds of behaviors that had worked so well last week. I complimented both partners for their hard work in therapy and commitment to their marriage.

Sessions 3 and 4. I assigned a weekly "date night." Each partner took turns planning the event.

Session 5. Katia and Seth reported a setback. The couple spent more time with Seth's friends, and Seth skipped the agreed upon date and family nights. The couple slipped into old behavior patterns and was discouraged. I used a metaphor of buying new shoes to normalize a temporary setback.

Therapist: Imagine you are window shopping, and then you see these great shoes. You really want to buy them because the comfortable old shoes you're wearing are worn and definitely need to be replaced. You try on the new shoes. They fit and look great, they're just what you wanted, and so you make the purchase. One day, you start to have pain in your heel. You take your new shoes off and see that a blister is forming. So for a few days, you put on your old shoes, long enough to let the blister heal. Gradually you are wearing the new shoes longer and longer and they become more and more comfortable.

My point, of course, was that change is, at times, an uncomfortable process.

I told the couple to go back to basics and do more of what had worked for them in the last few weeks.

Sessions 6 and 7. Seth and Katia were "speaking the same language" again and decided to terminate therapy after the next session. A one-week break was scheduled between Sessions 7 and 8 so I could feel assured that the couple was ready to terminate. The couple was given an assignment to bring something to the next session that was representative of the growth and change they had gone through during the past two months.

Session 8. In this final session, the couple reported that they were doing well. Katia and Seth both wore jeans to the session. Seth pointed at Katia's jeans, smiled, and stated, "I like that!"

The couple was playful during the session, complimenting each other and holding hands. Seth brought three roses to represent beauty, strength, and self-protection (thorns). More rosy metaphors: One of the three roses that was past its prime represented the past; another in full bloom, the present; and the third, partially closed, the future.

Seth: We don't know yet what the future will hold!

Katia: This is beautiful. This is the caring, wonderful, creative man I love.

Katia then pulled out a key crafted from the letters LOVE. She explained that their love is the key to their relationship. They exchanged gifts. I asked the scaling question about the quality of their relationship. Seth called it a 9, and Katia said 8.5. I made booster sessions available to the couple "as needed."

Katia: I thought it was so important to work with a counselor who was a foreigner, like me. Now I think what was more important is that you cared and respected both of us.

That felt good!

About four months later, Seth asked for a marital session. Katia had begun a B.A. in psychology and was pregnant with their second child. Seth had received a promotion that resulted in much traveling. They were concerned about how Seth's promotion would affect their relationship because his last promotion triggered conflict. We talked about ways to maintain individual, couple (date), and family time with Seth's schedule.

Seven months after this booster session, I received a greeting card from Katia confirming that the couple was doing well. Despite the arrival of their second child and Seth's promotion, they still managed to set time aside for each other.

◼ Outcome

The couple was seen for conjoint therapy for eight sessions and one booster session. It was not surprising to see that the couple responded well to the solution-oriented approach because they were bright, motivated, and well functioning. The variety of techniques used in this case (scaling question, Formula First Session Task, imagery) all worked well. Homework assignments, such as asking the clients to go out on dates, were successful. I used metaphors to normalize the inevitable ups and downs of the counseling process. I taught communication skills, and they picked up on them readily despite their cultural differences. I loved the termination ritual with the roses and the key. Beautiful!

Discussion

My husband is American-born, and we have, through communication, care, and love, developed a healthy marriage of 17 years. I believe that my own experience as an immigrant and leaving my family of origin and my country behind helped me understand Katia's needs. It is not essential for the clinician to have similar experiences to the client to be effective, but it offers hope to clients when they can see that the clinician has "been there."

It is not unusual that a couple like Seth and Katia will do well until a crisis or transition occurs. At such a time, cultural differences may add to the stress. I can easily imagine myself going through the same difficulty if my husband and I were to move back to my native country.

Biographical Statement

Karin Jordan, Ph.D., is Associate Professor and Director of the Graduate Department of Counseling at George Fox University and a Licensed Marriage and Family Therapist. Karin holds a Doctorate in Child and Family Development/Marriage and Family Therapy from the University of Georgia, and she is an Approved Supervisor of the American Association for Marriage and Family Therapy. She is the author of over 30 articles and book chapters and has extensive experience in working with culturally and ethnically diverse clientele. You can reach Karin at DrKBJordan@cs.com.

13

A Family's Grief

Connie M. Kane

Despite a life full of blessings, Connie Kane's client, a young married woman, was suffering from Generalized Anxiety Disorder with symptoms of irritability and insomnia. Kane started with individual therapy and then threw her net wider, including multicultural and family-of-origin issues. Medication brought relief from insomnia and freed energy for conjoint therapy. Painful family alliances were exposed as well as unresolved grieving. Honesty set this family free!

Sylvia came to see me a few months after I completed a master's degree in marriage and family therapy. I was working full-time as a family counselor in a community social service agency. Sylvia wanted counseling, she said, because she was "tired of worrying about everything and nothing all of the time." She explained that most of the time she found herself thinking that something awful was about to happen. She was 24 years old, married to "a terrific guy," financially secure, in good health, and about to apply for readmission to a junior college to resume studies toward a business degree. Despite these pleasant circumstances, Sylvia was tense, irritable, and tired from not getting enough sleep. Because she was thinking of returning to school, she hoped she could alleviate her anxiety and be free to concentrate on and enjoy her studies.

Sylvia began college immediately after graduating from high school but dropped out after one semester because she "always felt uncomfortable" in the classroom. Her grades were above average, and she could pinpoint no specific source of stress.

Sylvia was referred to me by a friend who had heard of me through another client. Sylvia was from a Mexican-American family and the fifth of eight children born to her parents. One brother, Jerry, born two years earlier than Sylvia, had died of leukemia when he was 17. Although only two of her sisters were still living with her parents, all of her immediate family lived nearby. Despite frequent contact, she felt estranged from her mother, her oldest brother, and three of her sisters. She had never felt close to them as she did with her father, Jerry, and her other two sisters. She believed that her mother considered herself superior to her father, although they came from similar socioeconomic backgrounds and Mr. Gonzalez had more education than his wife. Similarly, Sylvia believed that she and the siblings she was allied with were somehow in the "not-good-enough" camp.

Because my graduate degree was from a program that espoused in-depth therapy for family-of-origin issues with nearly all clients, I was immediately interested in Sylvia's family dynamics. The setting in which I worked was conducive to long-term therapy in that fees were based on a sliding scale and the number of sessions was unlimited. Sylvia, like most of my clients, did not use insurance.

Conceptualization

Sylvia's symptoms matched those of Generalized Anxiety Disorder. She had been experiencing excessive anxiety and worry for more than six months, found it difficult to control this worry, felt on edge and irritable most of the time, had difficulty sleeping, and could not identify a focus for her anxiety. The anxiety was severe enough that it interfered with her studies.

Sylvia described the impact of her anxiety on her marriage in two ways. On the one hand, she feared her irritability and self-absorption hurt her relationship with her husband. On the other, because he was patient and compassionate, she felt drawn to him all the more, which she believed deepened their closeness.

Sylvia was distressed about her family of origin. In tears, she spoke of her need for her mother's love and her desire to feel as important as her siblings who were closer to her mother. There seemed to be two coalitions within the family, one headed by Sylvia's mother, the other by her father. The latter included Sylvia. Sylvia perceived a definite hierarchy, with her mother's coalition holding the greater power. Neither Sylvia nor anyone in her father's subgroup could ever win her mother's unconditional love. Only the siblings in her mother's alliance were worthy. The father's coalition was left out of family decisions and told of family plans as an afterthought.

Some anxiety disorders respond well to medication, so I gave Sylvia the names of two psychiatrists. I believe that emotional and physical states can be significantly influenced by perceptions and belief systems, so I suggested family-of-origin work. She accepted the medical referral and agreed to begin therapy with a focus on family-of-origin issues.

Counseling goals were to alleviate her anxiety and resolve the tension she experienced in her family of origin, beginning with her mother. I chose Virginia Satir's Process Model, a family-systems approach that deals directly with affective expression among family members. Satir conceptualized family dysfunction as a blockage in growth aimed at maintaining family homeostasis, or balance. Satir believed that families opt for ineffective behavior because of deficits in their growth, specifically low self-esteem and poor communication. The necessary condition for change is the development of congruent, effective communication skills brought about through the actual experience of functional communication. Satir uses direct interaction with family members to model and teach effective communication. She affirms every family member through attention and acceptance and encourages the family to access its own resources and thereby enhance self-esteem.

I began with a family history and genogram to clarify family rules, roles, and relationship patterns. At the same time, Sylvia began using an antianxiety medication under the supervision of a psychiatrist. At the point that Sylvia was clear about the issues she needed to address and was able to speak about them in an assertive, nonaggressive manner, we would invite her mother to participate. The plan was to eventually bring in the entire family!

Process

Sessions 1–8. Sylvia worked with me individually. During the initial three visits, we constructed a genogram noting boundaries, tensions, alliances, and coalitions. We used the genogram to identify communication patterns and significant events. Two very difficult experiences stood out.

When asked about her earliest memories, Sylvia described an incident that occurred when she was between 3 and 4 years old. It was a school day for the older children, and Jerry was in kindergarten. Father was at work, while Mother stayed home with the young children. At noon Mrs. Gonzalez walked to the corner to meet Jerry's bus and walk him home, as she always did, but the bus was late, so she was gone longer than usual. Meanwhile, Sylvia grew frightened. She couldn't get out of the house to go after her mother and couldn't see her from the window. Sylvia worried that she was never coming back and started to cry. When her mother returned, she explained matter-of-factly that the bus was late and that there was nothing to cry about. Sylvia remembered wanting her mother to take her in her arms and comfort her, feeling both confused and hurt when that didn't happen. Her brother, on the other hand, patted her shoulder and said, "It's okay, Sylvie. We're all home now."

The second memory of note was that of Jerry's illness and death. Sylvia resented her family's inability to speak of what was happening at the time. She said she learned of his illness by piecing together observations of his physical symptoms, the strain in her parents' voices when they discussed doctors' appointments, and Jerry's refusal to comment when she asked him directly about it. She said that the fear she saw in his eyes when she asked struck her so deeply that she never posed another question, either to Jerry or to anyone else in the family. On the day he died, his parents returned from the hospital and told the children that he was "gone." Sylvia said she cried out, "Why?" to which her mother replied, "Leukemia. It was God's will." Those were the last words spoken on the subject.

Sessions 5–8. We addressed Sylvia's hopes and fears for conjoint therapy with her mother. Naturally, there was a close connection between the two: Her greatest hope was that her mother could, once and for all, dispel Sylvia's fear that her mother didn't love her; and her greatest fear was that, by the very act of asking for affirmation of her mother's love, she would lose whatever bit of it she might already have, plus the chance of ever having more. Since the realization of both of these depended on Mrs. Gonzalez's response, I had to help Sylvia see that she was giving up the power, as well as the responsibility, for the success or failure of the conjoint therapy to her mother, which left Sylvia feeling helpless and anxious. Then she recognized in this an old pattern and came up with an alternative scenario—to set goals for her own be-havior and to evaluate success according to her own achievement of those goals. Sylvia was like a child with a new toy and she couldn't wait to try it out! When she identified her greatest hope for the meetings with her mother to be that she, Sylvia, could be honest with her mother about her own feelings and her own questions, I knew we were almost ready to bring her mother in.

The last piece was to consider her goals for herself in the event that her mother would not respond as Sylvia would desire. On the day that Sylvia said that she would simply have to learn to accept her mother's feelings, however disappointing, I knew that the time had come.

Session 9. I asked Sylvia and Linda Gonzalez (her mother) to address the nature of their relationship, including Sylvia's doubts and fears about her mother's love.

Sylvia: (in tears) Mama, I'm not sure if you love me. If you do, I want to hear you say it, and I want you to show me.

Mrs. Gonzalez: (surprised and concerned) That's just not how I was raised, Sylvia. My parents didn't say that to us, and they didn't like it when they saw other people hugging and making a fuss over their kids. But I do love you. Of course I love you!

Sylvia:	But you spend more time with Sarah and Rosie. You invite them over or ask them to go shopping with you, but you don't do that with me. When I see you all together, you look like you're having fun. I don't know how to have fun with you.
Mrs. Gonzalez:	It is easier for me to be with Sarah and Rosie, and Robert, too. I'm not sure why. Maybe they are more like me, and you are more like your father. Sometimes I think you want something from me that I don't know how to give. But I love you just as much. (Both women are crying now.)
Therapist:	Sylvia, what do you want your mother to do to show her love for you?
Sylvia:	Just hug me sometimes, Mama.

And they did! They hugged and cried. Sylvia recounted the childhood memory of the bus incident. Linda didn't recall it, but neither did she discount Sylvia's memory. She told Sylvia she was sorry that she had been hurt by her unfeeling response. Linda made no attempt to excuse her own behavior. She said she didn't know if she would be affectionate and hug as often as Sylvia might want, but she assured Sylvia that she would never reject a hug that Sylvia initiated. That was acceptable to Sylvia.

Sylvia requested that we include the entire family in therapy, and Linda agreed. I stipulated that we should not include spouses of the married siblings for several reasons: (1) I wanted the immediate family to feel as safe as possible to address their common experience from the earliest stages of their shared lives; (2) including the spouses would have meant working with 14 people, which seemed unwieldy. I really thought nine was a bit much! In fact, there was simply no room in the office suite to accommodate 14.

Sessions 10–11. All seven living siblings and their parents participated. We struggled with differing perceptions of family dynamics, using family sculptures to illustrate boundaries and loyalties.

Sylvia:	Rosie, I want to know why you won't talk to me and what you and Sarah say about me behind my back.
Sarah:	Well, what do you and Rachel and Libbie say about her when she's not there? You don't invite her to your little gossip parties!
Rachel:	(interrupting) Gossip! Who was it that told Mama that I was dating two guys at the same time and was trying to get them to fight over me?

They interrupted one another, spoke for one another, and tried to outshout each other. They were reluctant to speak directly to one another about feelings, although Sylvia and her two younger sisters took some tentative initiatives in that direction. Mrs. Gonzalez agreed, when I asked, that she wanted the family to be closer and to be able to talk more freely and more respectfully. Easier said than done!

<u>Session 12.</u> Everyone was present. Sylvia began immediately.

Sylvia: I want to talk about Jerry. (a moment of frozen silence) I want to
                    know when he first got sick and how you found out about it and how
                    he died and why haven't we talked about him since and . . .

Her words were coming with great force and speed when they were interrupted with her mother's soft repetition of his name, "Jerry." As gently as I could, I asked, "What happened to your son, Mrs. Gonzalez?" She began to tell the story, beginning with his tiredness, his susceptibility to colds, the diagnosis, the choices, and finally, his death. Everyone was crying. Others spoke of what they noticed, when they first feared that it was really serious, and what they regretted in their behavior toward Jerry, particularly what they had not said.

Mr. Gonzalez: I couldn't talk to him about it because I didn't want him to be afraid.
                    I thought that if I acted like everything was okay that he would think
                    it was. But sometimes when he would look at me, I knew it was the
                    only thing we were both thinking about. I wish I could have told him
                    how much I wanted to make everything right with him.
Robert: That's exactly how I felt. And I hated seeing him getting sick and
                    weak, so I just stayed away.
Sylvia: I tried to talk to him, but he wouldn't talk to me. He just kept saying
                    everything would be okay, but I knew it wouldn't. Finally I got mad at
                    him because I didn't know what else to do. He's the one I counted
                    on, and he was going away!

Quiet tears, occasional sobs, and sometimes a hand on another's hand. Eventually, sighs and then silence, but not for long. They shifted to favorite memories of Jerry, to laughter, to more tears, and to more laughter. More sighs and more silence. After a pause that I hoped was long enough, I checked to be sure everyone was finished talking for the time being and then brought the session to a close, telling them how important I thought this sharing was and that I respected their courage and honesty.

<u>Sessions 13–15.</u> All nine attended. These last three sessions provided the opportunity for the family to work on their current relationships. Family members expressed the desire to drop their guard with each other and talk as openly about all aspects of their lives as they had about Jerry. They were listening more and interrupting less. They recognized natural alliances and discussed the possibility of supporting these without making them divisive. They agreed to convey messages directly instead of triangulating others and practiced this in session.

Among the more meaningful exchanges during these sessions was this dialogue between Mr. and Mrs. Gonzalez.

Mr. Gonzalez:	(looking at his wife) I don't know why, but I've always felt like I was failing you, like you wanted something from me that I couldn't give, but I didn't know what it was.
Mrs. Gonzalez:	(with tears in her eyes) I thought I needed to make you think that so that you wouldn't look down on me because I don't have as much education as you.
Mr. Gonzalez:	But that didn't matter to me! I always knew you were just as smart as me. You quit school to help your family and I respect that! Where could I have found a better wife and mother for my children?

My role was simply to facilitate communication. Sometimes that involved getting them to let one person have the floor without interrupting or shouting over each other. Other times, it was helping someone to name particular feelings and to express them directly to the appropriate person without accusing or attacking. I coached them to listen and then reflect what another had said without interpretation. It was hard work but it had become very gratifying.

Outcome

Sylvia reported relief from insomnia within two weeks after beginning the prescribed medication. At termination of counseling, she expressed confidence in her relationship with her mother and satisfaction and even joy with her family.

Honest and direct communication set this family free! That did not change the fact that members of the family naturally liked some of their children or siblings more than others, but they became more accepting, thereby reducing the resentment.

Sylvia came back for individual therapy two years later when her father was dying. Her major goal was to communicate honestly with him and the rest of the family. She was hopeful that the counseling breakthroughs about Jerry's death would help them now, and this proved to be true.

Before her father died, Sylvia told him of her love for him, her gratitude for his care and support throughout her life, her willingness to let him go, and that she would miss him greatly. He had been open with her, telling her about his process of accepting his own death, including the pain and fear, and thanking her for her contribution to the fullness of his joy. Sylvia described other family conversations in which her mother and siblings spoke directly with her father and with one another in a similar vein. The family was no longer keeping secrets. If they could talk about love and death, they could talk about anything.

Discussion

Although it has been 15 years, the Gonzalez family remains a vivid memory. They challenged me as few clients have. The first of these challenges was the intensity of emotion. Whether rage, fear, grief, joy, or love, expressed directly or indirectly, this family expressed emotion with great energy. Their silences were deafening. This family was an emotional tornado. Another challenge—facilitating interaction among nine family members—demanded considerable energy of me. I found that we required 90-minute sessions and that, afterward, I needed a 30-minute break to regroup before seeing another client.

Another difficulty for me was an apparent paradox: Family rules forbade open expression of certain feelings and discussion of sensitive issues, but family members displayed gregarious personalities and aggressive communication styles.

Our different cultural backgrounds presented an additional challenge. In my Irish-American family, we were expected to keep our feelings to ourselves. Emotional restraint and a high regard for privacy were prized. Self-determination was valued over reliance on others. Affection and emotional support were expressed only indirectly, through actions, rather than words. This wasn't really so different from what I saw in the Gonzalez family, but I had to keep checking myself to be sure I was being guided by professional standards rather than personal reactions. To help me with that, I discussed the case several times with my supervisor.

Another challenge in working with the Gonzalez family was that of maintaining realistic goals for therapy, in terms of who could be served and to what end. The more I saw, the more clinical issues surfaced. As might be expected, several of the married siblings, as well as the parents, were using the same indirect or closed communication patterns in their marriages, resulting in stress and dissatisfaction. I reminded myself that my client was the immediate family only. If couples wanted to enter into marital therapy, it needed to be with another therapist, preferably, after the family work was completed.

The depth of their work in therapy really impressed me. They accomplished second-order changes in their family system. That is, they changed structures, such as family rules about emotional expression and communication, and the boundaries between members and subsystems.

Some changes happened in response to family members' initiatives rather than mine. The most dramatic turning point was the interaction about Jerry's illness and death. Sylvia initiated that. She poked the hole in the dam that was holding back thoughts and feelings about the most painful event in this family's life. When the dam gave way, there was no rebuilding it, and family members poured out their emotions about Jerry, about their agony as they watched him grow weaker, about the aching need they felt to reach out to him and to each other, and regrets for not having done so. That moved naturally to vows not to make the same mistake again.

Looking back, I realize there had been opportunities to approach the topic of Jerry's death in each of the two earlier family sessions. Family sculpting had ignored Jerry, but I did not comment, perhaps because I was already struggling not to be overwhelmed by the intensity of this family's emotion, or perhaps because I hadn't fully grasped the necessity of their grieving together before they could be intimate in any other way. I am grateful that Sylvia courageously moved herself and her family toward healing.

Some interventions worked just as I had hoped. The antianxiety medication did give Sylvia sufficient immediate relief from her insomnia and anxiety to let her participate more fully in the family work. Individual therapy established useful goals for her relationship with her mother that led to conjoint therapy. I think it was probably a good move to start with Sylvia, then include Sylvia and her mother, and, finally, bring in the rest. Mama Gonzalez was the boss! I needed her on my side. To put it another way, I wanted Mrs. Gonzalez to have a vested interest in having the family therapy be productive. To put it still another way, the rest of the family needed Mother's permission to commit to counseling.

In hindsight, I recognize that this case taught me some important lessons. I had an inaccurate stereotype of Mexican-American families that this family challenged. Their reluctance to risk vulnerability and to express affection with each other showed me that even positive generalizations, such as that of expecting Mexican-American families to be open with one another, can limit my objectivity. Second, if I had it to do again, I would somehow have brought in a cotherapist. I wonder how much valuable material I missed by flying solo.

Humanistic theories of counseling hold that, given the right conditions, clients will know what they need to help themselves and will have the courage to accomplish it. The Gonzalez family affirmed the wisdom of this perspective. I treasure their memory.

Biographical Statement

Connie Kane, Ph.D., is a Professor of Education at California State University, Stanislaus, a family therapist, and an Approved Supervisor in the American Association of Marriage and Family Therapy (AAMFT). Her publications include: "African-American Family Dynamics as Perceived by Family Members," *Journal of Black Studies*, 2000; "Differences in Family-of-Origin Perceptions among African-American, Anglo-American, and Hispanic-American College Students," *The Family Journal*, 1998; "Using Dreams in Family Therapy," *The Family Journal*, 1997; and "An Experiential Approach to Family-of-Origin Work with Marital and Family Therapy Trainees," *Journal of Marital and Family Therapy*, 1996. You can reach Connie at ckane@bigvalley.net.

14

A "Selfish" Mom; A "Difficult" Teen

Bruce S. Neben

This case exemplifies the way brief therapy is supposed to work. Pragmatism rules. A limit of six sessions? Only one member of the family wishes to participate in counseling? No problem. Work with what you've got! Bruce Neben counsels a single mother to change her defensive response to her teenager's provocations. Her "surrender" breaks the vicious cycle.

Eleanor came to see me when I was a therapist and the clinical supervisor at an employee assistance program (EAP) for which she had benefits through her company, a textbook publishing firm. The EAP had contracts with a number of companies and governmental organizations to provide personal counseling for their employees. The counseling sessions are prepaid by the employers, and as such, the counseling was provided at no cost to employees. As with most EAP programs, the arrangement is for brief, time-limited therapy. Eleanor's benefit was limited to six sessions. The policy was to refer out to private practice therapists if the case was unresolved in that period. In her case, up to six additional sessions with a private practice therapist could be authorized. However, the expectation was that the EAP therapist (myself) would complete most cases within the given six sessions.

Eleanor was the divorced parent of a 16-year-old son, Jason. She complained that Jason was disrespectful, swore at her, and did not obey her rules. Jason was 5 inches taller than Eleanor, and muscular. She said she felt intimidated by him but she had never been afraid that he would hurt her physically. She recounted daily arguments in which they stood inches apart, yelling at each other.

Eleanor described Jason as "difficult to raise." She remembered him arguing ever since the divorce 10 years ago. She described him as stubborn and demanding. She had sought out therapists for help in dealing with him twice before, the last time two years ago, with little or no benefit. The last therapist had brought them both into the sessions and had tried to negotiate changes and agreements. Eleanor saw no progress in this treatment and finally gave up, feeling that she could live with things the way they were.

Things had become worse in the past year. Jason became more active in sports at school, trying out for several sports and eventually making the basketball team. She thought he was very stressed with the responsibilities of homework and basketball practice. At the same time, Jason's father, Carl, cut back visitation with Jason to one weekend and one weekday evening per month due to commitments to his second family. Carl had been seeing Jason an average of two weekends per month and one evening per week. Eleanor said Jason needed a break from her, and he needed to be with his dad more. I told her that although I was not a single parent, I could only imagine that raising a child alone must be difficult under the best of circumstances. I asked her if she enjoyed the breaks when Jason was with his father. She said she looked forward to those weekends when she could have some alone time. She was angry with Carl.

The divorce was angry and bitter. Carl had left the marriage to move in with a woman he met through his work. When Jason was 8, Carl and the new woman married and had children together.

Although she was angry with Carl, Eleanor said she tried to touch base monthly to work out parenting difficulties. She believed Carl did not understand the depth of the problems she had with Jason and did not do enough to help. Carl conceded that

Jason had become more irritable, but he said it was not a major problem for him, as he was able to handle Jason.

Jason was a junior in high school. He had several friends at school whom he would socialize with at the mall. Eleanor described his friends as "nice kids, good kids." His grades, usually A's and B's, had dropped a little lately. His last report card included C's along with the A's and B's. Teachers had not reported any behavioral problems. Jason had plans to attend the local community college after high school.

Eleanor wanted Jason in therapy to help him to become more cooperative and to "get out his anger." When I asked her how he felt about coming to see a therapist, she said she had not spoken to him about it.

■ Conceptualization

With reference to the *DSM-IV*, I first thought of Oppositional Defiant Disorder. However, by his mother's report, Jason's problematic behaviors occurred in interactions with his mother but not in school, so he did not meet the criteria. Some problems seemed to occur when Jason was with his father, but these were not seen by his father as significant. Jason did appear to have some problems with stress management and impulse control. I liked a diagnosis of Parent–Child Relational Problem because the problem appeared to be limited to the interaction between mother and son.

Who was my client? Or, whom should I bring into the office? In cases like this it is occasionally useful to bring the father into the therapy, especially since the indications so far were that he had more success with Jason than did Mom. What's more, father and mother could learn to work together to Jason's benefit. Jason would see that even though his parents were divorced, they held a "united front." But, as Eleanor reported that she and Carl had an adversarial relationship, it was unlikely that this approach would be productive. For his part, Jason wanted no part of therapy. He didn't think he had a problem. I, therefore, decided to see Eleanor alone. If that plan didn't produce positive results in three or four sessions, I would insist that Jason come to a session and, perhaps, try a different tack.

There are some limitations of working with only one family member. The therapist is only hearing one side of the story. For example, if I had brought Carl and Jason into my office I might discover that Eleanor exaggerates, is histrionic, unreasonable, or otherwise inaccurate. While it is true that each family member has a different perspective, hearing all sides does not necessarily help the therapist solve the problem. Therapists come up with their own version of the truth, and there is no guarantee that the composite or psychologically informed version is any closer to the truth than any other. I think the therapist's job is not to search for objective truth—which may not exist—but to help the client solve problems, and that process can begin with one family member. In this case, I chose the course that I saw as most straightforward and efficient.

It could be argued that bringing in only one family member limits the effect of the treatment. If two members come into the treatment, the therapist has twice the chance to affect the system. However, when other members are not motivated to participate, my philosophy is, "Work with what you've got."

This approach to family therapy is in step with the practices of the Brief Therapy Center of the Mental Research Institute (MRI), which I highly value. Unlike other family therapy approaches, the social focus here is narrowed and limited. The "strategic" focus stays on the family, but the "tactical" focus is on individuals or small groups of family members. A major factor in the decision of whom to see in the therapy is based on the assessment of (1) who is most motivated to take action to solve the problem; and (2) who has influence in the system to make changes. Individuals who are unmotivated may interfere with therapeutic suggestions. Willing clients provide the therapist with "elbow room" to initiate change.

Process

<u>Session 1.</u> I asked Eleanor to give me more details, specifically, "Who said what to whom?" and "What happened when . . . ?" She brought up many problematic interactions stated in generalities. I stopped her and asked her to describe the last upsetting situation and what was actually said, as if she were an impartial observer.

Eleanor replied that when she came home from work a couple of days ago, she and Jason had a typically angry interchange, which I will reconstruct here:

Jason:	I'm going out.
Eleanor:	Where do you want to go?
Jason:	The mall.
Eleanor:	Why don't you stay home this afternoon?
Jason:	I really want to go; everybody will be there.
Eleanor:	I don't think so.
Jason:	Why not?
Eleanor:	(becoming irritated) You know why not. I want you to stay home and do your homework. You need to spend time on your schoolwork; your grades need help.
Jason:	I can do my homework later, after dinner.
Eleanor:	You might not. You should do your homework now.
Jason:	(angrily) You're a selfish bitch!
Eleanor:	(angrily) Don't call me that! (more calmly) Listen, you know your grades have slipped, you know you need to study. I can't do it all for you.
Jason:	(loudly and angrily) Who asked you to? You only think about yourself. You are a selfish bitch.
Eleanor:	(loudly and angrily) I hate that. Stop it. I work all day for you, I feed you, I put clothes on your back. This is the thanks I get? You're the selfish one. You don't know what it is to work hard and be tired at the end of the day. You want to go to the mall? When do I get to go out with my friends? When do I get to have some rest? Some fun? You're a spoiled punk.
Jason:	(yelling and coming closer) I'll do what I want; you're not my boss.
Eleanor:	(yelling) Go to the mall. You'll do as you want anyway; you never listen to me.

Jason left the house and went to the mall, returning at 8 P.M. He rummaged around the kitchen to get his supper, then did some homework and went to bed at 10 P.M.

Eleanor said that the above was a pattern: Jason would ask for permission to go out with friends; she would say no; he would call her a selfish bitch; she would defend herself, then angrily surrender.

I suggested that instead of bringing Jason into the treatment now, we should first see what could be done without him. She agreed.

I asked Eleanor what she had tried to solve the problem. I didn't want to suggest an approach that had failed. She said that she had tried not to yell and tried even harder to convince her son that her views about the importance of homework were in his best interest. She tried to defend herself against his charge of selfishness. But nothing she had tried was successful.

I asked what others had suggested. Her mother told her to remind Jason that if he wanted to go to college, he needed good grades. No effect! Eleanor's responses to Jason's ongoing challenges were "more of the same." I hear this story from many parents who consult with me about their kids.

We spent the rest of the first session discussing what it meant to her to be selfish and whether she agreed with Jason that she was selfish. She did not agree. I made this intervention:

Therapist:	It sounds as if your situation is frustrating. I have some ideas, but they are not fully formed. Would it be okay with you if I just thought out loud for a few minutes?
Eleanor:	That would be okay.
Therapist:	I was wondering what would happen if, when he called you "a selfish bitch," you simply agreed with him. I'm not suggesting that you are selfish, but what would he do if you agreed instead of arguing or defending?
Eleanor:	I don't know. I have no idea.
Therapist:	I'd like to propose an experiment to help us to more fully understand Jason and his reactions in various situations. I need more information.
Eleanor:	Sure, anything that will help.
Therapist:	This might be difficult, but I think you can do it. When he accuses you of being selfish, say to him as if you were terribly curious, "You might be right. Maybe I am a selfish bitch." Then walk away.
Eleanor:	I think I can do it.
Therapist:	I need to know exactly how he responds.

Session 2. A week later, Eleanor arrived looking worried. She had done her homework: "You might be right. Maybe I am a selfish bitch." Jason demanded to know what she meant. She thanked him for helping her to learn something interesting about herself, and sat down, appearing to be deep in thought. Jason left the house, returning an hour later to do his homework and eat. There were no other arguments

that week. Eleanor was concerned that his anger was still there and that the arguments might resume. I asked her what might bring up the arguments again, and she said she didn't know. She also said that it would be helpful if Jason spent more time with his father. Much of the second session was occupied with discussing Jason's and Eleanor's relationships with Carl.

I suggested that she think of ways to reduce stresses on Jason and continue last week's experiment.

Session 3. Eleanor reported that she had done something "selfish." She had gone out to lunch with a friend, something she had not done in a long while. She had also called Jason's father and had spoken with him about spending more time with Jason, which he agreed to do. I asked her how she had avoided a fight with Carl. Eleanor said that in the past she would become defensive with his accusations and criticism. This time she just refused to argue. She stuck to her points and the discussion went reasonably well.

Session 4. Eleanor reported that things were better. Jason spent the weekend with his father.

Eleanor:	I think you were wrong all along. I am not a selfish person. I just want to do what is right for my son.
Therapist:	I did not mean to suggest that you are selfish. Of course, you act in the long-term best interests of your son. I'm curious. Tell me how it felt to tell him that you are selfish.
Eleanor:	I resented it at first, but then it was interesting. It seemed to stop his arguing. I've realized that I don't need to convince him that he has to study. He won't admit that I'm right. It's okay with me if he studies behind my back even if he doesn't concede my point.
Therapist:	Makes sense.
Eleanor:	Luckily, I have some support from Carl now, although that may change at any time. It won't last.
Therapist:	If problems come up with Carl again, is there anything you can do to increase the chances that the discussion will go well?
Eleanor:	I need to not allow myself to be drawn into an argument.
Therapist:	How do you do that?
Eleanor:	Just stick to my points.
Therapist:	Hard to do.
Eleanor:	Well, he can be a jerk, but I know he loves Jason. I need to remember that. If he criticizes me, I will just remind myself that he is a jerk. What he says about me doesn't matter. He's not my husband anymore.
Therapist:	This might sound a bit odd, but if you, for some strange reason, wanted to start arguing with Jason again, what would you have to do?
Eleanor:	If I spent more than a couple of sentences trying to convince Jason that I am right or let him get my goat by insulting me, we might start

arguing again. Not getting hysterical when he called me a selfish bitch took the power issue out of it for him. And for me.

I suggested that she ask Jason if there are things that he could do to keep things on track.

Session 5 Eleanor reported that the waters remained blessedly calm. She had not spoken with Jason as I had suggested, afraid that if she raised the issue his anger might come back. I conceded that she knew him better than I did and she should do what she thought best.

Eleanor was pleased that Jason had invited some friends to his house for the first time. She wanted to continue therapy after our six sessions to make sure things continued to improve. I proposed that we stop now after five and keep a session "in the bank." She could return to use her last session if a problem came up that she couldn't manage on her own. Then if she needed more therapy, we could make those arrangements. She was agreeable to that plan.

Outcome

Follow-up Telephone Call I had not heard from Eleanor in six weeks, so I called. She said that she was content that the arguing between her and Jason was now in the normal range. Jason told her that he liked the cutback on arguing. On occasion, they watched TV together. Jason seemed to be studying more, but she couldn't tell yet if his grades had improved. She felt no need for another appointment and thanked me for my help. I haven't heard from her since.

Discussion

Regardless of how it started, Eleanor's arguing with her son took on a life of its own. Her arguing maintained the behavior, as it is difficult for one person to argue alone. My strategy was not to determine who was right but to break the vicious cycle. Success with Jason led Eleanor to apply the same principle to the disturbed relationship with Carl. Small changes, initiated and nurtured, result in larger, broader changes.

The key is to discover precisely what people are saying and doing as they attempt to solve the problem. The next step is to direct the client to do something different. In this case, Eleanor became upset when her son called her a selfish bitch; she took the insult to heart and proceeded to defend and justify herself. This approach failed repeatedly. As long as Eleanor "honored" Jason's accusations, the arguments escalated. Additionally, Eleanor gave in to Jason's demands out of guilt and fear. Jason learned that yelling pays. The reinforcing aspect of the client's capitulating when her son yelled guaranteed that the violent arguments would continue. When Eleanor conceded to Jason that she indeed might be selfish, the insult lost its energy, its potency.

Eleanor mistakenly understood my directive to mean that I thought she was or should be selfish. In retrospect, perhaps I could have been more clear. It worked, anyway. Insight was not the goal. The goal was to help the client end the arguments.

Traditional therapists assume that insight must precede behavior change. I have found that insight primarily occurs as a consequence of behavior change.

To prevent a relapse, I asked Eleanor to consider what could go wrong that might result in a return to previous painful symptoms: "If you, for some strange reason, wanted to start the arguing again, what would you have to do to get things back the way they were before?" It is a question that often leads the client to wonder for a moment how truly sane the therapist is. But it also makes more concrete the client's own contribution to the problematic relational system.

In the fifth and last session, instead of referring out to another therapist to help her to continue her progress, as she requested, I suggested a session "in the bank." Here I was implying two things. First, problems are normal and can be expected regardless of therapy. Second, the real hope and expectation is managing these inevitable problems on her own. I kept the door open if she needed to return, thus creating a psychological safety net. In hedging about her request for a referral, I assume that less therapy is better than more therapy. The longer clients are in therapy, the more likely they will become dependent on the therapy. The sooner therapy ends, the more likely that clients will credit the changes to themselves.

I used my follow-up telephone call to extend the effects of therapy beyond our sessions. I gave credit for the change to Eleanor. After all, she was the one who had the courage to face the problem and take the risks necessary to change.

At the time I saw Eleanor, I was married and a parent of young children. Like Eleanor and most parents on the planet, I also struggled with the conflicts of work and family. I had not yet experienced the challenges of raising teenagers.

Biographical Statement

Bruce S. Neben, Psy.D., lives in Portland, Oregon. His interests include the problems of couples and families and the interactional aspects of depression and anxiety. Bruce has a clinical psychotherapy practice and provides supervision and consultation to other therapists. He is a board member of the Oregon Board of Licensed Professional Counselors and Therapists. You can reach Bruce at neben4@attbi.com.

15

Mr. and Ms. Blah

Patrick O'Malley

Patrick O'Malley sized this couple up as a dream case, ideal candidates for marital therapy. They were young, well educated, and verbal. But the outcome was a divorce. O'Malley makes sense of this poor result by inventing a new label, "insufficiently bonded couple." He maintains that when couples miss out on an early developmental experience (in this case, falling in love) they bring severe limitations to marital therapy. O'Malley's case study raises important questions. Where are the diagnostic categories that could help us understand marital problems? For all of its hundreds of descriptors of individual psychiatric problems, the DSM-IV has little to say about relationship problems.

Michael and Andrea were a marriage therapist's dream case. They were young, educated, attractive, and verbalized their concerns with ease. Michael and Andrea had been married for four years, were in their mid-20s, and were building professional careers. They were referred to me by more than one person, and consequently, they had confidence I could help them. They paid cash for services rendered, so I didn't have managed care to contend with. I anticipated doing some good work with this couple.

In the initial session, both, cited concern about the marriage as the reason they sought counseling. My intake form has a checklist of problem areas. Michael checked depression, vocational direction, marriage problems, sexual concerns, and self-doubt. Andrea checked only marriage problems.

Andrea and Michael described a growing distance in the marriage. They described their first two years together as generally satisfying but with some arguing. For the past two years, they had become distant and the arguing had increased. Andrea had stopped including Michael in her social life. Their sexual relationship had declined into nonexistence.

After 15 years of doing marriage therapy, their story was not unfamiliar, but something about this case didn't ring true. Although Andrea and Michael stated that they had been arguing, their affect was flat. No energy. The arguments were contrived. Most fighting couples exhibit plenty of energy, albeit negative energy.

Conceptualization

The marriage was my patient. Neither Andrea nor Michael showed symptoms that would justify an individual diagnosis. Neither "pathologized" the other as the unhealthy one. They each functioned well in their respective worlds outside the marriage. Their stated concern was the distance in their relationship.

The obvious behavioral manifestation that brought this couple to counseling was arguing. But their description of the arguments somehow lacked authenticity, and I suspected that the problem was deeper. There was more to it than a power struggle or poor communication skills. Even in the first session, I realized that Michael and Andrea lacked any real attachment or bonding. My task was to help them develop a bond to one another that perhaps never existed.

I planned a therapy strategy: take a thorough history of their courtship; investigate the marriages they experienced in their original families; and give assignments to increase meaningful contact. I would use cognitive, psychodynamic, and behavioral approaches.

In my previous work with couples who have not bonded properly, there are usually important cues to be found in their dating histories. I ask about their courtship to develop a point of reference for the original dream they had of their lives together. In couples that lack a healthy bond, the energy of romantic love is often missing, yet they continue in the relationship and eventually marry. What leads them to marriage?

What kinds of marriages were Andrea and Michael exposed to in their original families? Unattached couples may lack a model. I want to know about the negative and positive images of marriage they carry.

To couples that need to add energy to their marriages, be that positive or negative, I give homework to educate, motivate and create interactions that are useful for our sessions. To couples struggling with attachment, I hope the assignments will create momentum. I want to nudge these couples into interaction that is missing in their daily lives. Their compliance or resistance to these assignments gives me a lot of useful information.

Process

Session 1. I routinely ask couples to tell me of a time when they were happy. Most couples will express pleasure about their courtship or the first years of marriage or living together. The best Andrea and Michael could come up with was that they didn't argue very much in those early years. There was no reminiscence about romance.

Michael and Andrea explained that they weren't alone when they dated. Most of their time was spent with various groups of college friends. Group activities continued in the first two years of marriage, but then Andrea went back to school and no longer had time to socialize with old friends. Then the arguing increased. There was no bond to support the relationship when their group broke up.

This worried me. Didn't they talk about personal and intimate subjects when they dated? They could not remember doing so. Did they get to know one another when they were in the group setting? They had not. The group went to clubs or bars that were not conducive to intimacy. I asked if they had any other interests they shared that created a sense of closeness, and they could think of none.

I explained to Andrea and Michael that my tentative theory of their marital difficulty was that they did not accomplish the developmental task in the early stage of their relationship of forming an attachment. The emotional glue was insufficient to keep them connected at times when they were experiencing stress. They did not know what to do with each other when they were alone. They were, I said with attempted humor, like a "one trick pony."

Michael and Andrea accepted my hypothesis. I proposed that we retrace their steps to the missed milestone. Perhaps they could recall the early sparks that ignited the relationship and expand their repertoire of ways to connect. We would also attack unproductive communication habits.

I was pleased with my summation of their dilemma and my gentle invitation to work on their relationship. I also knew that I had not had much success with other couples who had presented with no evidence of early attachment. Somehow, I hoped to discover a breakthrough approach with this "unbonded" couple.

Andrea: I'll have to think carefully before committing to marital counseling.

Michael affirmed that he was ready for counseling but he did not want to push Andrea to do anything she wasn't ready for. They agreed to talk it over and get back to me.

I have seen several hundred couples and conducted thousands of hours of marriage therapy. Rarely do I see a couple that does not agree to come back at the conclusion of the first session. Although I believe it takes some skill to process a couple's description of their marital problems in a balanced manner, the main reason couples come back is that they simply have more to say than they get out in one session. Granted, what clients want to talk more about is how their spouses are not meeting their needs. The point is that there is *energy*, even if the energy is negative.

In my training as a marriage and family therapist, I was exposed to theories of how individuals come to select one another and form a bond that leads to a committed relationship. Individuals may choose each other based on a sense of the other completing them. They may pick someone who is equally differentiated from their family of origin. They may have a more dynamically based drive to choose someone with whom they can work out the unfinished business from childhood. These theories of mate selection do not address the possibility of insufficient attachment. In situations when couples feel forced to marry or in cultures where there are arranged marriages, I would expect a lack of attachment, at least initially. But of course, the marriage of Michael and Andrea was neither forced nor arranged.

How do couples miss out on the stage of romantic love that forges the bond required for a growing viable relationship? I began to think about other couples, particularly in the age group of Andrea and Michael, who lacked attachment. I thought I might be onto something. I looked through my files for couples in this cohort group to see if I could discover similarities.

Andrea and Michael were "Generation-Xers." As a baby boomer, I was mildly distressed to learn that here were people from a generation younger than mine! Though younger, the Xers were old enough to need marriage therapy. I read about their sociology and demographics. They came of age during the years of exploding divorce rates. Between 1965 and 1977 the divorce rate doubled. More than 40 percent had lived in a single-parent home by age 16. There was another interesting piece of sociology. In my youth, I suffered through the rough-and-tumble of spontaneous and unplanned neighborhood adventures and relationships. But thanks to media-enhanced violence, parents of Generation-Xers placed their kids in safe, adult supervised activities—soccer, orchestra, gymnastics, trombone lessons, and so on. Safe, but lacking in opportunities to learn how to initiate relationships.

Generation-Xers marry later and put off having children. They fear repeating the patterns they saw in their divorced parents. Of course, not all couples in this group exhibit attachment problems, but many describe a similar courting ritual of being in a group when they dated. I wonder if this dating style inhibits intimacy and if supervised activities prevent opportunities for building one-on-one relationship skills.

Session 2. Several months passed before Michael and Andrea returned. They wanted to try four or five sessions and then evaluate progress.

Through the years, I have collected material that can serve as "homework" for couples. The packet of material I sent Michael and Andrea included several worksheets that couples can fill out and verbalize to one another. My favorite in this collection of exercises defines intimacy in 17 categories. The instructions ask couples to check whether they have enough, too much, or wish for more of each type of intimacy. Categories include emotional intimacy, financial intimacy, sexual intimacy, work intimacy, and spiritual intimacy. This exercise helps couples set goals for where they want their relationship to grow.

I sent some of my marital worksheets to Michael and Andrea in the mail. Their assignment was to complete two sheets a week. I directed them to carefully listen to the other talk to gain more knowledge of each other.

Session 3. Michael and Andrea brought their completed intimacy inventories to the next session. They generally agreed on the areas in which they wanted to experience more closeness: emotional intimacy (sharing feelings, emotions, joys, and sorrows), goals intimacy (sharing personal and marriage goals, plans, and hopes), recreational intimacy (sharing hobbies, sports, fun times), and working intimacy (sharing housework and other work). This was a hopeful sign. Although this session was productive, the flow of interaction was like molasses. I felt as if I was overcompensating for the lack of energy in the room. A mentor of mine once told me to be wary about working harder than the clients. I was verbalizing twice as much as both of them put together.

I gave Andrea and Michael the assignment of working on their emotional intimacy. They agreed to spend 20 minutes daily talking about their day to each other. I directed them to talk about their emotions. Were they frustrated, happy, sad, disappointed? Andrea would take 10 minutes while Michael listened, and then they would switch. As couples progress with this assignment, I tell them to share things beyond and deeper than the events of the day.

Session 4. I was seeing Andrea and Michael every other week. I give couples enough homework to keep them engaged in working on their issues during the two intervening weeks. My experience with the couples I have seen with an insufficient attachment bond, like Andrea and Michael, is that they rarely follow through with assignments. True to form, Michael and Andrea did the exercise only a couple of times over the two weeks. They said that they did not find the exercise difficult. I asked them to talk about how they experienced one another during the exercise. Silence, dead space between them. They had done the exercise in a mechanical way. Their difficulty in making contact was obvious to all three of us.

I changed direction and asked them to describe the marriages they had watched while growing up. I wanted to know what imprint of a primary relationship they brought to their own marriage.

Andrea's parents had divorced when she was in elementary school. Although she recalls her parents having fought, she didn't realize how bad things must have been. After the divorce, she and her siblings visited their father every other weekend. Both parents remarried, but Andrea did not form a strong bond with either stepparent, although these relationships weren't especially troublesome.

Michael's parents were still married. He saw his parents as modeling healthy behavior. They did not fight and were responsible and predictable. Neither showed much emotion or affection. Michael wished they had been more effusive, but this was his only complaint.

I asked both Michael and Andrea to write their thoughts on their personal vision of a healthy marriage. I wanted them to take the categories of intimacy we had discussed, plus the positive and negative aspects of their parents' marriages, and develop a picture of the relationship they desired for themselves. Couples who develop a healthy attachment to one another usually discuss their dreams about their marriage in courtship. They talk about how they want their marriage to be and how they do not want it to be. Healthy attached couples may stray from their vision, but the vision remains as a compass point.

Session 5. Michael and Andrea followed through with the "vision" assignment. Their composite picture of a healthy marriage included friendship, affection, reliability, emotional support, strong attraction, sharing the work load, having fun, planning a future, and being parents. Although Andrea and Michael had done a good job, there was a heavier than usual depressive mood. Andrea said that the exercise made her sad. In focusing on what she wanted in a marriage, she realized how hopeless she felt that she could have such a relationship with Michael.

Andrea's comment brought me back to the root of the problem. She honestly declared doubt that Michael was the right choice for a spouse. Although Michael showed more interest in working through marital problems, he did not argue. He was resigned to the possibility of the truth Andrea was revealing.

In couples who have momentum toward change, therapeutic exercises may be painful but useful in dislodging marital logjams. Although Andrea's awareness increased as a result of this exercise, the new information increased the sense of hopelessness.

Our therapy contract called for one more session. Although I did not see any last-minute marital conversions taking place, I did have one more idea. I sent Michael and Andrea home with a Myers-Briggs test to take and return to me before the next session. I give the Myers-Briggs, a personality-type assessment, to almost every couple I see. It's useful in showing couples that many of the differences they struggle with and blame each other for are simply a consequence of how they are "hardwired" differently as individuals. Often I have seen couples quit personalizing the differences between them when these benign differences are explained.

Session 6. In the last conjoint session with Andrea and Michael, we reviewed their Myers-Briggs results. On the Extrovert-Introvert scale, both Andrea and Michael were on the Introverted side of the continuum. This indicated that neither partner was likely to initiate a conversation!

After reviewing the test results, Andrea announced that she and Michael had talked it over and decided separation and divorce was the only viable plan, given the distance they both felt. Michael again stated his desire to work on the relationship, but he would honor Andrea's wishes. I offered to assist them in separating and divorcing. Because they had been married such a short time and had no children, they did not believe they would have much difficulty.

Michael stated that he would like to come for individual sessions. I told them that individual counseling would be an option for each as long as they understood the confidentiality limitations. I do not reveal any information gained in individual sessions to either spouse after marital therapy is terminated.

Michael returned for several more sessions. He showed only minor signs of grief. Andrea did not return, and I heard nothing from her after the final conjoint session.

I saw Michael 11 times during the next year with the goal of finding a healthy relationship. He began to engage in new relationships soon after his divorce was finalized. He was keenly aware of whether his date was finding him attractive but gave little attention to how attractive he was finding her. He had difficulty being assertive with the women he dated. His concern with hurting the feelings of women inhibited him from defining his needs.

Michael's growing insight into relationship patterns was useful in identifying the difficulties he had in his marriage with Andrea. We theorized that his excessive "other" focus distorted his discernment about the level of attractiveness he was experiencing. He determined that although Andrea fit several categories of attractiveness, he never experienced a *primary* attraction to her. She was pretty, educated, and shared the same friends. But there was no "chemistry."

Outcome

The divorce went through without a hitch. Michael ran into Andrea from time to time due to their common friendships. He described these encounters as pleasant and friendly. He experienced neither anger nor sadness.

Michael finished individual therapy with a belief that he had learned about himself in relationships. He had entered into several short-term and uninspired dating relationships. He was more assertive. This skill helped him to disengage from a relationship sooner when he became aware it was not viable. He left counseling with confidence that he would find the right woman. I did not hear from him after he terminated counseling.

Discussion

A tough marital case triggers my fear of inadequacy more quickly than any other therapy failure. I can conjure the dread of seeing such a couple by just viewing their names in my appointment book.

Michael and Andrea were an example of a particular subgroup within the group of lifeless marriages. Most low-energy couples are worn out by conflict. Their strong original bond is frayed by a long pattern of frustrating behavior. Their individual differences aren't accepted by one another. They seek help after they have used most of their emotional energy defending themselves.

The insufficiently bonded couple lacks the original reference point of an experiential attachment. They describe the relationship as "missing something" or "empty." They never fell in love! Couples who miss this developmental stage describe having used a checklist approach in their selection of one another. Their mate had attributes that outweighed obvious liabilities. There was no "blind" love in the equation.

I do not bring any personal experience from my marriage to working with poorly bonded couples. My courtship with my spouse, Nancy, was full of romantic love. We were young and we fell hard for each other. In 24 years of marriage, we have felt the bond stretched thin, but it has been there as a safety net when we traveled too close to the edge of marital calamity.

I have not seen the subject of insufficient bonding described specifically in professional literature. The notion of attachment theory as applied to couples is, itself, relatively new. John Bowlby, a psychoanalyst, postulates an instinctive drive for intimate connections from infancy to adulthood. Children and adults function with resiliency in a stressful world as long as they are connected with a trustworthy other. Therefore, our psychological survival is enhanced or threatened, depending on the quality of the marital bond.

There is a fundamental question with regard to couples like Michael and Andrea. Can a couple that lacks a primary attachment be helped to develop one? I do not believe they can. The psychobiology of attachment may not be able to be constructed after the fact. An analogous circumstance is the real limitation stepparents experience when trying to bond to their spouse's child. While they may be able to develop a functional relationship and emotional closeness, they can never experience the level of attachment that grows between parent and infant child. The earlier they come into the child's life, the higher the chances for a deep bond.

Even though the lack of a primary bond may not be repairable, not all of the couples I have seen with this dilemma have chosen divorce. Some make the best of it. Such couples develop their relationship at a friendship level, although the emotional intensity is missing. Often, the deciding factor influencing these couples to stay together is whether they have children.

I have worked with couples in which one spouse claims to have attached strongly and the other did not. The attached spouse explains the distant behavior of his or her partner with some reason other than poor attachment. When the dynamic of insufficient attachment is revealed to the attached spouse, there are feelings of betrayal. The attached spouse feels duped.

With the benefit of hindsight, I worked too hard to draw this couple out because their lack of energy raised my anxiety. When I do this, I feel as if I am cheerleading the couple rather than following their cues. I would like to go at the pace set by the couple. Questions that focused on their current experience of the session would have helped.

I have seen other unbonded couples. Although I have questioned the value of doing therapy with them, they have expressed appreciation of my work. Those who separate and divorce benefit from knowing that they tried counseling. Those who stayed together did so with more understanding of the distance between them and were able to engage in some new behaviors that narrowed the gap and capitalized on strengths.

Attachment creates a safe harbor from the hostile environment in which we live. Marital therapy explores and repairs the attachment between partners. As evidenced by Michael and Andrea, when that bond is nonexistent, spouses may leave each other to search for another with whom they might connect. As Michael left after his final session, I wished that both he and Andrea would discover the extraordinary experience of attachment.

Biographical Statement

Patrick O'Malley, Ph.D., is a licensed marriage and family therapist in private practice in Fort Worth, Texas. He is a clinical member and approved supervisor of the American Association for Marriage and Family Therapy. Pat authored a chapter in *Case Studies in Child and Adolescent Counseling*, 2nd edition (Prentice Hall, 1998). He also coauthored "A Day In The Life" (*Journal of Systemic Therapy*, Winter 2001). Pat can be reached at pomalley@swbell.net.

16

Beyond Stalemate: Steps to Intimacy

Vimala Pillari

When Vimala Pillari met this couple, an attempt at marital counseling had failed. Individual counseling for both partners cleared the way for a second and successful round of marital counseling. Success meant that each of the partners was able to use the insight gained in individual counseling to shake loose from dysfunctional childhood relationship patterns. The capacity of relationships to heal and promote personal growth is beautifully illustrated.

R on and Sally were constantly fighting. At Sally's insistence, they began marital therapy. After only a few sessions, the couple decided to pursue individual therapy because they could not even sit together through a session without fighting. Barry, their marital therapist, observed that Ron overpowered Sally with anger and sarcasm. Barry had given up on a conjoint approach. He continued to see Sally in individual counseling and referred Ron to me. Barry told me that Ron would benefit by being seen by a female therapist. Although I prefer to help troubled couples together, I took on the case. Barry and I agreed to future conjoint sessions as needed.

At that time, I was employed as a therapist in a family service agency. Presenting problems and client population were diverse. Child abuse, marital problems, and adolescent and elderly issues were frequently heard. Fees were paid on a sliding scale basis. Because Ron did not wish to use his insurance, he paid a nominal fee based on his income.

My sessions with Ron and, later, with Sally lasted for about two years (obviously, they were not managed-care clientele).

Ron was tall and unusually slender with a flowing beard and piercing brown eyes. He had been a history professor for nine years before changing fields to become an artist and self-employed businessman. Ron organized exhibitions where he sold his own art and that of other artists, as well as antiques and collectibles. Sally was tall and slim with sandy blonde hair and hazel eyes. She was an interior decorator.

Conceptualization

Ron reported to me that he feared intimacy and was too rigid. He had a history of violating the rights of his wife or anyone with whom he had been in a close relationship. In intimate relationships Ron would become controlling, verbally abusive, and emotionally distant from his partner. He would transform from a charming lover to a "control freak," criticizing everything that his partner did. At this time, the only object of his criticism was Sally. I decided on a mild *DSM-IV* diagnosis of Adjustment Disorder. My hope was that if Ron could better cope with stress and anxiety, his conduct would improve.

Ron admitted that he had dated his students while he was a professor. After living with a particular student for seven years, they moved together from California to a small southern town. One day he came home to find a note from her. She had just walked out of his life permanently, taking her belongings with her. Her only explanation was that she had never wanted to move to the South in the first place. He was hurt and angry but became engrossed in his new position.

True to his pattern, Ron became overly friendly with a married student, Sally, who had two teenage daughters. An undergraduate student in her late 30s, Sally aspired to become an "intellectual." Her husband, Charles, a down-to-earth construction worker, hated reading and would rather watch a football game or boxing match on television than participate in any form of intellectual discussion. Dissatisfied with her marriage, Sally unburdened her problems on her professor friend, Ron. Ron gave her a soothing shoulder to cry on. Shortly after, Sally divorced her husband and married Ron.

Though supportive and understanding throughout their friendship, Ron suddenly built emotional walls. Sally would later describe this change as follows: "He became a stranger with dark moods and a bad temper, and he was secretive and private." Sally moved into Ron's house and sold hers. According to their prenuptial agreement, Sally had no rights to his house or any of his belongings. Ron reminded her that his house was fully paid for, and Sally had to ask permission to decorate or move her own things around in the house. This rankled Sally because she was an interior decorator! The only rooms she could redecorate even minimally were the kitchen and her side of the bedroom. The living room and other rooms, including the bathroom, were out of bounds. It was *his* house, and Sally felt like a guest. Her older daughter was away at college, and the remaining teenage daughter, Michelle, had ugly verbal fights with Ron when she wouldn't comply with house rules. One day he locked her out of the house. After that, with Sally's help, Michelle moved to her father's house in the same neighborhood.

Finally, I brought Ron and Sally into marital therapy. I used Bowenian family therapy because I heard both Ron and Sally constantly reflect on their unhappy childhoods, including a pattern of triangulation. I think that Murray Bowen does a great job of helping therapists understand family-of-origin issues.

Process

In my first few private sessions with Ron, he expressed anger in such statements as, "Sally is always suspicious of me. I married her, though I was not the marrying type." Meanwhile, Sally was anxious for a joint session, so the following week, Ron, Sally, Barry, and I met together. Sally was teary-eyed throughout.

Ron: (furious) This is the way she is; she gets to people by crying and makes everyone feel sorry for her.

I turned around and asked Sally if this was actually a strategy, as Ron implied.

Sally: No, no it isn't!
Ron: (smirking) There she goes again.

I asked Sally why she was weeping, and she said that there were " too many things not right in my life."

Ron: (bellowing) *Tell me* what they are right now.
Therapist: Excuse me, Sally is talking to me.

He sat back reluctantly. I decided at this point that if I saw them in joint sessions, I would use the Bowenian method of routing communication through me.

Sally and Ron agreed that they wanted to see me again, and Barry was more than willing to bow out. He felt as if he were on a merry-go-round with them and was out of patience. So I took over the case.

In my joint and individual sessions with Ron and Sally, I heard their stories. Earlier, Ron had told me that Sally did not trust him. Sally also told me that Ron did not really trust her. When she discovered him talking to some woman on the phone for a long time and questioned him, he accused Sally of being absurdly suspicious. He simply had several women friends in whom he would confide or who would confide in him.

Sally: He could be very understanding and would stay on the phone for two hours or more, but he'd never talk to me about his friendships or conversations.

Everything in the house was marked "his" or "hers." If Sally accidentally touched Ron's things, he would curse her. Often, he would scold her as if she were a child.

In my sessions with Ron, I came to understand that he came from a family in which "you shouldn't show your feelings; feelings were a weakness." Ron remembered being bitten by a dog as a child. He was flabbergasted by his parents' businesslike attitude as they drove him to a hospital. He was hurt by their lack of emotion. Many years later he heard his younger brother mention that their mother really had been frightened, but as she had run to the bathroom crying, having seen Ron bleeding from the dog bite, their father yelled, "Control yourself." Ron was happy to find out about this incident because it showed that his mother cared. During adolescence, Ron would protest his family's quiet dinners because he wanted to discuss matters of current interest. When he pushed, his father's belt, pulled out like a whip, put Ron in his place.

Ron's mother was involved in an affair for several years from the time Ron was 13. His father did not confront her about it, but Ron did after he finished high school. Then the affair stopped, apparently as a result of his confrontation. In retrospect, he believed his mother depended more on him than on her husband and, in turn, Ron looked out for her.

Sally could never recall getting compliments from her mother. The oldest of four children, Sally played surrogate mother to her siblings, as her mother was usually ill. Although Sally did a great deal of housework, cooking, and cleaning, her mother never thought she did a good enough job of taking care of her siblings or doing school work. Her father was more supportive when he was available. Sally remembers spending hours in front of the mirror on her prom night. She wore a pink formal dress. Her mother said, "Sally, you look pale and dull. I'm sure your classmates will shine by comparison." Sally was crushed. Her mother was very critical of her and succeeded at finding faults.

Sally and Ron replicated family-of-origin roles in their marriage; they played complementary roles. Ron liked taking care of a woman in a controlling manner, and Sally was dependent and in need of approval. As a trade-off it worked, but the lack of intimacy was obvious. Ron would revert to treating Sally like a student. Their money remained separate in individual savings accounts, although there was a joint account for groceries. They ate out often at Ron's favorite restaurant (of course), and each paid his or her own tab. They even used separate bathrooms in the house. If Ron bought toilet paper for Sally's bathroom, he left the receipt on the kitchen table, expecting reimbursement. These events didn't take place because Sally was incompetent to handle money, as she maintained that she had handled the finances in her first marriage.

In individual sessions, Sally complained that Ron had changed after their marriage.

Sally: Ron had been a caring, loving confidante with whom I could share
                my secrets and problems, but now we are strangers living in the
                same house.

Sally believed that Ron constructed careful boundaries to avoid intimacy. This
was how marriage was modeled in his family of origin.

An incident occurred that offered me clues about their relationship. Ron had
kept a journal in which he had written every day for 20 years. Sally secretly read his
journal and later confessed out of guilt. In the joint session that followed, Ron called
her a "motel whore," a "tramp," and the like. Sally immediately took the one-down position and cried. My attempts to empower her were fruitless.

And yet they were committed to marriage counseling. Sally and Ron told me
that they wanted to "work on our marriage." I asked Ron why he pushed Sally away.

Ron: When we have fights, which is all the time, Sally puts down my family.
Sally: He does the same with me.

Ron told me about an incident that had occurred four years before. They were
in bed fighting, and then Sally ran naked out the front door and drove away! Ron panicked because he was afraid that she would get into an accident or get arrested. She
returned safely in 10 minutes. Sally said that she had felt overwhelmed in the argument but agreed not to repeat this behavior and had not. But Ron kept throwing this
episode back at her.

When they fought at home, Sally retreated to a corner in the kitchen in *his*
house and slept on the floor. He forbade her to sleep on the living room couch. They
were living in a zoo, and Ron was the keeper.

Ron was warm toward outsiders until they became part of his personal life, at
which point he would hide behind his professorial persona. He rapidly withdrew from
intimacy. When I asked him to account for his fear of intimacy, Ron explained that his
tears, fears, and shame were laughed at while he was growing up, so he learned to
keep his feelings under control and to strive for control in close relationships. Even
the expression of positive, nurturing feelings meant being too vulnerable. From her
family, Sally carried a sense of defeat and inferiority into her relationships.

I alternated between individual and joint sessions. After they had individually
worked at developing a clear awareness of their own issues and at developing a sense
of self, I gave them tasks to perform as a couple. For example, I directed Ron to
"allow" Sally to decorate the house, except for his study. Sally, in turn, was to proceed
without asking his permission. After a few weeks, I asked about the results.

Sally: At first I was scared to do anything in the house without his permis-
                sion, but in short order I forgot about all of that and started having fun.

Ron: I felt very reluctant to let her do the decorating initially until I saw
                what a great job she was doing and how much more cheerful the
                house looked.

But when I asked Ron if he had told her, he said he hadn't. When I asked why, Ron responded with a rare twinkle in his eye directed at Sally, "You know that I liked what you did." Sally agreed that she did.

Therapy became a joy ride. I assigned other tasks, including holding hands while talking to each other about pleasant, uncontroversial topics. Ron started introducing his friends to Sally, and she did the same. They went out on dates together.

I suggested that Sally tell Ron about her ideas for decorating *his* antique shop. Ron employed her as his decorator. Eventually, Sally ran part of her decorating business out of Ron's antique store. This saved money and gave them time together. Increasing affection and mutual business interests paved the way for a successful joint venture.

There was also more involvement with each other's families. Ron had been estranged from Sally's daughter, Michelle. But on her occasional visits from college, Ron and Michelle found a shared love of collectible books.

The couple was responsive to any communication task assignment. They decided to see me every other week and then once every three weeks. The positive momentum led to a decision to sell Ron's house and buy one together, a meaningful move.

Outcome

I love this statement from Ron: "I'm not the marrying type, but in spite of myself, I made the right choice in marrying Sally." Sally learned to be less diffident in their relationship and worked hard at extricating herself from the one-down, "student" position. An effective therapeutic technique was to enable down-to-earth discussions about home, work, and planning for the future with Ron, thereby creating a scenario in which she could stand on her own. This kind of discussion played to Sally's strengths and enhanced her self-confidence. With Ron's emotional support and overt expression of love, she blossomed.

Most of the pair's ability to be intimate started with understanding their own family histories and diligently working on their own issues, which eventually led to openness, vulnerability, and true intimacy. The actual behaviors involved in creating a new home, and then being appreciated for those behaviors, solidified Sally's gains. As Ron recognized his rigidity, this created openings for Sally to try her wings. As Sally flew successfully, this encouraged Ron to be more flexible. This is the kind of interactive momentum I pray for!

Discussion

To work through life's issues and problems, regardless of life's trials and tribulations, is to learn to communicate, to be aware, to work on your boundaries, and to sustain intimacy. Being intimate requires mutual risk. If you are in a one-way relationship, in which only you express intimacy, you will feel shame and develop deeper patterns of dependency. When you attempt to share your deepest thoughts and feelings but are rebuffed by your partner, you are bound to feel hurt.

Growth is a lifelong process. Everyone, given a chance and the right atmosphere, can blossom. However, like different flowers, each one of us, depending on the rain and sunshine we've received in our families of origin (our roots, if you pardon this endless metaphor), will grow at different levels and at different points. This whole process often can be accelerated with an awareness of the need for help.

I reflect on my own close relationships and how my experience prepared me for a therapeutic relationship with Ron and Sally. I came from a stable home, where every family member's rights were respected, even as children. There was a great deal of affection, and verbalization of problems was encouraged. I was happily married to a man who was sensitive, cared for me, and looked out for my needs and desires, and I reciprocated. On the one hand, these idyllic circumstances offer me little or no insight into complicated and dysfunctional relationships. On the other, thanks to a strong foundation, I bring a realistic vision of how respectful and loving relationships can work.

Thus, I helped Ron and Sally move towards an egalitarian marriage. It is not often in my experience that clients work hard enough to reconstruct their dysfunctional relationships. Their total commitment to the marriage and their desire to work at their relationship resonated with my own idealism about marital therapy.

Biographical Statement

Vimala Pillari, DSW, LCSW, is both dean and professor at the Graduate School of Social Work at Dominican University. She is a licensed clinical social worker who has specialized in counseling with culturally diverse populations. Her recent books include *Shadows of Pain: Intimacy Issues and Sexual Problems in Family Life; Human Behavior in the Social Environment: The Developing Person in a Holistic Environment; and Human Behavior in the Social Environment: Families, Groups, Organizations, and Communities*. You can reach Vimala at vpillari@email.dom.edu.

17

Time Wasted or Time Invested?

Thomas Scofield

An unmarried, childless couple seeks counseling because of poor communication. Scofield provides a useful discussion of diagnostic nomenclature. He diagnoses his identified patient as having an Adjustment Disorder. Then he refers to the DSM-IV's Global Assessment of Relational Functioning Scale for a far more meaningful diagnosis that incorporates the couple's communication style.

Starting with "self as instrument" as the basis for a positive therapeutic relationship, Scofield exposes how family-of-origin issues, such as birth order, influence current patterns of communication. Look for a surprise ending!

T his unmarried, childless couple sought counseling for what they described as poor communication. Both were undergraduate students in their mid-20s who were living together. Linda was working towards a degree in health care; Mark, in business. They were referred to the Advanced Marriage and Family Practicum (AMFP) by Linda's therapist at the University Counseling Center, who recommended marital counseling. The AMFP is staffed by advanced graduate students in marriage and family counseling. There is no charge for counseling.

Mark had previously met with his pastor, who also suggested conjoint counseling. When first interviewed, both said that if something didn't happen quickly, they would go their separate ways.

■ Conceptualization

The couple told me about difficulties with communication, and they questioned the viability of their relationship. There had been a recent breakup. The difficulty was later defined as the couple's inability to openly express opinions without the fear of getting the other's "nose bent out of joint" or becoming overly sarcastic. Arguments only served to emotionally isolate them from one another, so they wished to avoid arguing. They were also confused.

Mark: We have trouble interpreting what the other one needs.
Linda: I have a hard time understanding what he's feeling or meaning.

Mark's fear of abandonment led him to be submissive. As I reviewed the in-session process, I could see that Mark desperately tried to be whatever it was that he thought Linda wanted him to be. Although I never directly challenged it, I felt there was a theme of control in his mannerisms. Of the two, Linda seemed stronger and more comfortable with leaving the relationship if things "got ugly." What Linda had the hardest time with was Mark's desire for increased emotional intimacy. She vacillated between "on" (pursuing) and "off" (distancing).

Linda: I initially chased after Mark. Yet when we got together, I found myself in need of emotional and physical space.

As Linda went after this space, Mark pursued. Although Mark had been involved in other intimate relationships, Linda had not. Mark's previous relationships had failed because, as he said, "My girlfriends couldn't commit."

Fortunately, there were no mandated reporting or other legal concerns. Neither client was taking medication. Linda reported that she had sought counseling in 1990 following a suicide attempt in which she had mixed hard liquor and prescription medication. She denied any current suicidal ideation.

I decided that Linda, the identified client, met the characteristics of Adjustment Disorder with Mixed Disturbance of Emotions and Conduct. I based this on the couple's recent breakup (psychological stressor), their intense arguments, and Linda's depressed mood and anxiety.

The Global Assessment of Relational Functioning Scale (GARF) rates relationships on a continuum of 1 (disrupted, dysfunctional) to 100 (optimally functioning)(American Psychological Association, 1994). Using the guidelines provided, I rated the couple's relationship at 57 primarily because their communication was frequently inhibited by unresolved conflicts.

I sketched out a rough genogram for each client's family of origin to uncover similarities and differences. One difference was that Linda was the youngest of two children, having a brother, age 26, who was four years older than her. At 24, Mark was the eldest of two siblings, 10 years older than his sister. I'm interested in how birth order accounts for interpersonal style. Mark's parents were about 40 years of age, and Linda's were about 50. This could actually account for differences in parenting style and modeling.

Using the genogram, I asked about family-of-origin communication and conflict resolution styles.

Therapist: How did you react when family members fought?
Linda: I never saw my parents fight. There was plenty of conflict, but it was never resolved.
Mark: I would get very angry and usually leave the situation if there was an opportunity to do so.

These responses spoke to poor early modeling of conflict resolution skills.

Therapist: How have rituals or traditions regarding conflict resolution in your family of origin impacted you to the present day?
Mark: I now have a need to talk *immediately* after a conflict to ensure everything gets settled.
Linda: I close down, shutting out everyone.

Obviously, these dynamics created barriers.

I try to stay in the "here and now." I am not keen on applying ready-made techniques. Having been trained by professors who studied, practiced, and modeled an experiential approach, I, like them, am highly active. I lean toward a constructivist view when trying to understand the problematic descriptions my clients offer.

▄ Process

Session 1. Mark and Linda channeled communication through me, so my first intervention was to have them sit directly across from one another. They struggled with how best to describe their difficulty. I thought I would use imagery. I had never done this before, but it made sense.

Therapist: (to Mark) Close your eyes and see yourself floating downstream past words and phrases that might name what you think is causing difficulty. Can you see yourself floating, drifting?

Mark:	Yeah. (eyes closed, smiling)
Therapist:	Let yourself drift and settle very softly upon a word or a phrase.
Mark:	Passion!
Therapist:	That was quick!
Mark:	That's what she brings out in me. (Mark provides a reassuring glance toward Linda and touches her knee.)

After a brief discussion about how Mark's passion might have created nervousness and indecision for Linda, I asked Linda to do the same exercise.

Therapist:	Linda, I wonder if you could close your eyes now and see yourself floating past words and phrases. Can you see yourself doing this?
Linda:	Yeah. (smiles and looks directly at Mark) I don't want you to look at me while I do this.
Therapist:	I'll make sure he doesn't look. (laughter) Now let yourself drift and settle very softly upon a word or a phrase you might come to.
Linda:	Excitement! The excitement of it all because this is my first committed relationship. This is all new to me.
Therapist:	Cool! He peeked though. I did my best to stop him, but he looked anyway. (laughter and the two look at one another) Did it happen too fast? I mean when you first tried to capture one another?
Linda:	It scared me. We didn't know how to express ourselves to each other. His passion overwhelmed me because I didn't understand it.

I wanted a better picture of what was *not* being talked about. There were stylistic differences in the way both approached or avoided conflict.

Therapist:	(looking at Linda) Could I role-play Mark for a bit? And Mark, you come over here and be me, a detached observer. I'll do my best being you, but I don't think I can talk as softly as you. (therapist and Mark switch chairs, and therapist talks to Linda as though he were Mark) What do you want me to know?
Linda:	You mean my feelings about all of this?
Therapist:	(talking as if he were Mark) Yes, I want to know how you feel.
Linda:	That I'm not going to give up on our relationship.
Therapist:	(talking as if he were Mark) That's what I've feared the most. That you were just going to give up and I'd lose you.
Linda:	I can see that because it's happened before. I can see how you would see it that way.
Therapist:	(talking as if he were Mark) It scares me that we can get to that point. When you pull away my initial reaction is to try and fix it, poke and prod until you give me whatever it is that I'm looking for, until it's the "in-your-face" kind of thing.
Therapist:	(as therapist) Is that fairly accurate?
Linda:	Very.
Therapist:	How do you want it to be different? (motions to Mark to switch back to his own chair)

I decided to role-play Linda as well. (The therapist motions at Linda to switch chairs.)

Linda: Oh, so you're going to be me now?
Therapist: It only seems fair. (laughter)
Therapist: (talking as if he were Linda) This is new for me. It probably feels as if I'm just putting my toe in the water. I need some space, some breathing room, so I can find out for myself where we can connect.

I sent Linda back to her own chair. Switching roles enabled me to expose covert feelings without Linda and Mark being personally accountable. Toward the end of the session, I picked up on how Mark did not take personal ownership of his thoughts and feelings. Many times he would refer to his ideas and beliefs as though they were shared by both him and Linda. So I asked him to use the personal pronoun "I" and gave him some examples. I also provided material on differences in gender communication styles.

Session 2. I summarized the first session and asked Linda and Mark about the direction they wanted to go. The conversation turned to exploring how Linda and Mark got their needs met.

Therapist: Mark, of the two, you seem more quiet and introverted.
Mark: To a point. There are times when I'll stand my ground, but with her I'll give in.
Therapist: How come?
Mark: I guess I'm kind of a pushover. (laughter)
Linda: He wants me to think I've won.
Mark: I'm a little more of a thinker.
Therapist: Manipulative? (Linda laughs.)
Mark: (looking at Linda) That's not true, I'm more . . .
Therapist: Deceptive?
Mark: Yeah, that's a better word.
Linda: I like *manipulative* better than *deceptive*.
Mark: I intellectualize things.
Therapist: Turn them a little bit? (therapist rotates index finger and thumb clockwise then counterclockwise)
Mark: Just change them a little bit so they come up the way I want them to.

In this exchange, I had stumbled onto some interesting stuff. Most of what I discover comes by the way of serendipity.

The session bogged down when the couple talked about perceived difficulties in the relationship. Again, standing in for them allowed me to get a better feel for how the couple's conversations got muddled.

Therapist: (talking as if he were Linda) You know it hurts me when you say things like that. It's like you don't think, you shoot your mouth off.
Mark: I apologize. I should have said that I was hurt, too.

Therapist:	(talking as if he were Linda) Your apology is accepted. But this is something that constantly comes up when we argue.
Mark:	I'm not sure what to say. I need to try harder to control the things that I say instead of taking cheap shots. I should take a deep breath or something.
Therapist:	(talking as if he were Linda) You're going to try to do things differently, right?
Mark:	Yes!
Therapist:	(talking as if he were Linda) What do I do that makes you jab at me like that? What is my part?
Mark:	I try to talk and get things out, and you always say, "I don't know what to say." I hear that a lot from you, or it's just silence on the other end of the phone. I can't handle the silence.
Therapist:	(talking as if he were Linda) You know that it takes more time for me to process things. Why is silence such a big deal?
Mark:	If you don't respond even when I push, that's when I start getting sarcastic! By then, I've reached the boiling point.

Interesting dynamics! Before we ended, Mark seized an opportunity to go further.

| Mark: | I'll give you a chance right now. Because, honestly, right now as soon as any conflict comes up, you're really quick to throw up your hands and say, "I knew it, just forget it." It bothers me a lot that you don't give me a chance to change. I want a chance to take a situation and make it better. I want you to give the things we learn in counseling a chance to work. |
| Linda: | I understand that now! What I'm saying is that I just wish I could communicate with you like we do here! I know you would like those questions and all that interacting. |

As the session came to an end, the couple had clearly begun to gain resolve by "hanging in there" with one another.

Session 3. Check-in time to see if we were all on the same page. I restated that therapy is all about what changes the clients wanted and how committed they were to achieving them. I told them I was impressed with their willingness to remain open and tolerant of my style. I affirmed the hard work they had done both in and out of session.

The presenting problem, though still centered on relational issues, drifted to Linda's parents and their not-so-subtle attitude toward the couple, particularly Mark.

| Mark: | (speaking directly to Linda) It annoys me how your parents tell you what you need to do. (an extended period of silence) |
| Therapist: | You both have a fine gift for gab tonight. (laughter) |

Mark asked Linda if his involvement in her struggles with her parents pushed her further away. She indicated that the irritation with her parents made her feel unstable, and that made her lash out at Mark.

Linda: (speaking directly to Mark) But when things like that happen, we both get resentful. We take it out on each other. I don't really realize that I'm doing it until it's too late.

Therapist: Mark is a safe target. You trust enough in your relationship that he wouldn't take a hike. Because I don't know if you could get that upset with your parents and trust that they would still be there.

Linda: No, I couldn't with them.

Mark picked up on something that told him Linda was not telling him the truth. Rather than ignore it, he confronted her. The whole exchange afforded me an opportunity to question how it was that Mark assumed things rather than offering tentative interpretations.

Mark: You know what you said earlier when you could tell from her eyes if she liked your suggestions or didn't like them? I can read her eyes, too, and that's how I can tell that she's not telling me everything.

Therapist: Okay. That's a good awareness. But notice the difference in how I stated it, what I actually said.

Mark: You said you saw something and you weren't sure what it was and you wanted to be sure.

Therapist: Right, all I did was tell her what I saw. I didn't inform her about what it meant. I didn't say, "I know you're not telling me the truth." I wanted her to know that I saw something in her eyes, but I didn't know what it meant.

Session 4. I was doing less now as they took more control of the sessions. I would offer opinions from time to time and listen for opportunities to facilitate. I asked if anything more had come out of their reading about gender differences in communication.

Linda: It's like when we get into an argument, I just kind of . . . I really don't know how to explain it. He's more rational, I suppose, than I am.

Therapist: Are you feisty?

Linda: Kind of. (Mark smirks.) What was that?

Mark: Just a reaction. (laughter)

Therapist: (jokingly) Listen young man, while I'm trying to talk to her, don't you be pulling any crap over there.

Mark: I didn't do anything. (Mark shrugs his shoulders apologetically.)

Linda: Okay, I'm feisty. (looking at Mark) And you're smirky.

These folks had developed a sense of humor, or mine had rubbed off!

Therapist: Did you notice her reaction?

Mark: She said it in a kidding way, but I know she doesn't like it when I smirk.

Therapist: If we were to put it on the "crummy things to do" scale with 10 being very crummy, you'd (to Mark) probably put it at a 1 or 2, and my guess is it was probably a 5 or 6 for Linda.

Mark:	Yeah, you're probably right.
Therapist:	Linda, I find your perception of yourself as melodramatic intriguing. From what I've seen and heard, it seems more like sensitivity than melodrama. It's like you personalize his actions immediately. For example, if he chuckles or smirks, it feels like he's driving a stake through your heart. Maybe I'm being melodramatic.
Linda:	No, I'm sensitive to a lot of things he does, maybe too much so.
Therapist:	You're both sensitive but in different ways for different reasons.

Session 5. I began our fifth session by affirming that Mark and Linda had become more aware and immediate in handling conflict. They were making progress with some sticky issues with Linda's parents.

Therapist:	How could we best use our remaining time today?
Linda:	I believe that it's no use for Mark to talk to my parents because I know exactly how they'd treat him. They'd pretend they understand, and then when he walks out the door, it would be like, "He's still a jerk." They wouldn't see any change.
Therapist:	They don't see their daughter's immaturity? It all falls on Mark?
Linda:	No! They find fault with me too.
Mark:	It makes it hard to be around them. When Linda was admitted to the nursing program and then made the dean's list, her mom said, "What else are you going to do, because you're not going to make it in nursing." It just about killed Linda.
Linda:	My mom just didn't believe I could maintain good grades despite my initial success. She has it set in her mind that I can't make it!
Mark:	It's always been like that, and I've always tried to compensate, to fix things for her. (pauses for a moment) I think I'm just going to bite the bullet and do something about it.
Therapist:	That's quite a metaphor. You'll need to be careful which way the lead is facing so you don't shoot your mouth off or blow holes in your arguments. (laughter, after a pause) At any rate, the metaphor tells me that "fixing it" for Linda means suppression of feelings for you. She may not even want you to do or say anything. It may be something you both want to talk about. What's the next logical step? I think that's something I'll send you home with.

Session 6. At our sixth and final session, the couple stated they were satisfied with how they had progressed. Linda no longer waited to tell Mark what was on her mind. She discussed her concerns immediately, absent of any fear that things were going to get out of hand. They had opted for comfort before, for staying connected at all costs, at the expense of taking risks, at the cost of disregarding needs. Now Linda was taking chances.

Mark needed less reassurance with regard to immediate conflict resolution. This allowed Linda to feel more in control. As Linda became more confident in openly expressing her emotions and needs, Mark's anxiety and fear of abandonment subsided. A vicious circle had been replaced by positive momentum.

During the terminal phase, the presenting problem had shifted from the couple's arguments to the nonaccepting posture of Linda's parents toward Mark. The clients had decided to concentrate on the positives of their relationship and support one another. Linda saw her parents as rigid and, along with Mark, had decided not to try to force a change. At this writing, the couple has completed a six week follow-up, and they continue to be happy with their progress.

◼ Outcome

When I reflect on this case, I realize a significant piece of information came my way in the second session, when I discovered that Linda had been a "party girl with an attitude." Mark qualified Linda's statements, saying, "She can hold her own and swears like a sailor." This was a very different image from the timid and submissive young wallflower she portrayed herself to be previously. Linda immediately endorsed this observation, "That's right! I want to be accepted for who I am, and I don't want someone telling me how I'm supposed to be." This clearly upset Mark. He feared that he couldn't handle such an assertive person. Later, they told me about an argument that escalated into screaming and the throwing and breaking of objects. I came to see both partners as spontaneous and assertive, as well as outrageous, and used this knowledge to their advantage in subsequent sessions.

Therapist:	You got on the floor and screamed?
Mark:	Yeah! And kicked walls.
Therapist:	What? Like on all fours? I'm trying to picture this.
Mark:	No, I said we threw stuff on the floor. (laughter)
Therapist:	Oh, I'm sorry. So what, you both acted childishly? Kind of had a simultaneous temper tantrum?
Linda:	Extremely! It was extremely immature and childish.
Mark:	That did it for both of us. We had crossed over the line.
Therapist:	What did the episode mean?
Mark:	We had been trying to hurt each other.
Therapist:	It sounds like a lot of frustration had been building.

I was surprised by the way the whole thing turned out. Usually, I encounter more resistance, and the counseling process, at times, seems like it is going nowhere. In this case, we moved forward. Why? I modeled interactions that promoted the likelihood that all of us would work with, rather than against, one another. I poked fun at Mark and Linda and they returned fire. Humor encouraged humility and flexibility. We did more of what worked and less of what didn't. I was careful not to conceptualize the presenting difficulties or clients as pathological and thereby reduced blaming.

Discussion

This case affirms my "self-as-instrument" view of counseling. I am resolute that a positive therapeutic relationship is a must with regard to positive therapeutic outcome.

I permitted myself to be surprised, puzzled, and astonished by my clients' stories and by how discoverable unknowns can be put to use therapeutically. To some degree I think my marriage of 21 years played a positive role. My wife doesn't hesitate to take a stand with me, holding me accountable, yet staying close and committed. In my marriage, I've learned how conflicts can be resolved in a constructive way. I've also learned to be humble.

There was one thing in this case I would have done differently if I had the chance to do it again. I would have used videotaping. I could have highlighted certain aspects of the in-session videotaped material so the couple could see how their interaction was changing over time or, better yet, how their conversations got bogged down.

Having said all of this, I must relate the following. In the early part of December 1997, I encountered Linda, quite by accident. After a brief exchange regarding her current coursework and progress toward her degree, Linda disclosed that she and Mark were no longer together. Although the relationship improved during counseling, Mark continued to place unacceptable demands on her. They separated following Mark's ultimatums about how the relationship "should" be. Linda saw little hope for reconciliation but said that she and Mark were on friendly terms and supportive of one another. If that were not surprise enough, a day later Linda's mother called to tell me that Linda was feeling better than she had in a long time. Mom told me that Mark had been controlling and wanting every moment of Linda's time. "Linda has simply blossomed since leaving him! She's back to her old self."

Humility! The final and ultimate lesson.

References

American Psychiatric Association. (1994). *Diagnostic and statistical manual of mental disorders* (4th ed.). Washington, DC: Author.

Biographical Statement

Thomas Scofield, Ph.D., is an associate professor in the Department of Counseling and School Psychology at the University of Nebraska at Kearney. He is a board certified, licensed professional counselor. In conjunction with the university's counseling center, Tom coordinates and provides clinical supervision for the Advanced Marriage and Family Therapy Practicum. He is senior author of "Marriage and Family Training: Relating Training to Changes in Behavior, Case Conceptualization, and Therapeutic Outcome" (*The Family Journal*, 1997). You can reach Tom at scofieldt@unk.edu.

18

The Speed Demon
and the Backseat Driver

James N. Sells

The identified patient is a successful businesswoman, a community activist, and an elected member of the city council. She is also in trouble with the law and has just been released from a psychiatric hospital. She suffers from dissociative episodes, anxiety, and depression.

Sells uses an object-relations paradigm. The marital relationship is the context for addressing childhood pain, existential angst, and stress.

*C*athy remembered the patrol car's red and blue lights.

Trooper: Evening ma'am. Did you realize your speed as you drove into the valley?

Cathy: No, I really wasn't paying attention.

Trooper: In this state ma'am, the maximum speed limit for an undivided highway is 55. You were going 70. May I see your driver's license, insurance papers, and registration? Thank you, ma'am, I'll return in just a moment.

Cathy gripped the steering wheel. She was panicked. Another speeding ticket. It was 1:30 A.M., and Cathy had no idea where she was, when she had left home, or why.

When the trooper returned with the ticket, Cathy was shaking so badly she could not respond to his questions. She could only cry. The sobriety test indicated that she had not been drinking. Then came the ambulance and the phone call to her husband: "Thomas, I'm sorry. I did it again. I'm so sorry."

Cathy contacted me by phone after being referred by her psychiatrist. She described the speeding ticket incident during our first session. Cathy was a 46-year-old Caucasian, a respected businesswoman who owned several small clothing shops, and an elected member of the city council. She had just been released from an inpatient adult psychiatric hospital. She was recovering from a series of dissociative episodes, anxiety, and depression.

I work at a suburban private mental health agency that employs the full range of mental health professionals, including psychiatrists, psychologists, counselors, marriage and family therapists, and social workers. As a licensed psychologist, I see about 10 clients per week, mostly couples, and a few individuals and families. This part-time practice complements my full-time position at Northern Illinois University.

Cathy came for her first appointment the day after leaving the hospital. Hesitant speech and fidgeting indicated anxiety, which she acknowledged. She said she was not afraid of therapy but was fearful that she would lose everything if therapy failed. Cathy wanted to convince herself and me that she was not "nuts." I felt pity as she described the mess she was in.

Cathy had been arrested for speeding six times in the previous two years. Her road trips were unplanned and dangerous. After a bad day at work, a fight with her husband, or a political battle in a council meeting, she would find herself in another state, at the side of a highway with a trooper asking for her license. She had no recollection of how she arrived or where she was going. The most recent incident resulted in the suspension of her driver's license. The news was in the paper and the gossip line sizzled. City council opponents were having a field day. "Can this person be trusted to conduct city business, given that she seems to have a few *votes* missing?" Old friends became former friends. The resulting depression was rooted in her loss of control over both her mind and her body and shame at the destruction of her reputation.

▪ Conceptualization

I use an object-relations paradigm. My model has three steps: (1) observation; (2) validation; and (3) collaboration.

Observation. I observe the couple or each individual's interactions to see how he or she elicits behavioral and emotional responses from others. This process of eliciting roles is called *defining projections.*

Validation. The second step is to uncover the usefulness and limitations of the above relational projections or styles. This is accomplished by validating the client's current style as being useful in meeting fundamental needs but frustrating and inefficient in meeting current relational demands. The way of being learned in childhood was expedient to acquire our need for security and significance. In adulthood, it may become restrictive. For example, a child learns to get help by making demands in a "squeaky wheel gets the grease" style of family politics. In a marriage, this outspoken "child" is in conflict with a spouse who finds such behavior to be childish and rude. What was at one time a useful way of surviving is now limiting.

Collaboration. Finally, I help clients develop a broader range of relational skills to meet each other's needs. Partners act as counselors toward one another, and their relationship becomes the context in which to address childhood pain, existential angst, and the stress of life. I help them understand each other's past as a means towards creating new patterns.

Cathy was pleasant, confident, and articulate, but she was running (or, more accurately, *driving*) from something. What about the dissociation, finding herself behaving as another person? Was this an initial sign of the complicated self-splits consistent with a dissociative identity disorder? Was there a lack of conscious awareness of her actions? Was there some sort of relationship between Cathy's outrageous behavior and her need for relational safety, security, and significance? What was the effect of her actions on her marriage and her family?

Cathy had been married to Thomas for three years. Two prior marriages ended in divorce. She married her first husband in college because she became pregnant. The marriage lasted for two years. Cathy's son from this first marriage was 23 years old and lived in another state. The marriage to her second husband lasted 10 years. He was employed by an oil company and was out of the country in three-month blocks. When they were together, they fought. When he was transferred to the corporate office in another city, Cathy refused to relocate, and they divorced amicably.

Cathy had racked up years of therapy beginning in young adulthood. Her primary issues had been anxiety associated with business pressure and depression subsequent to failed marriages. There had also been childhood abuse, neglect, and emotional abandonment. Her mother, a school principal, had unrealistic expectations of her to perform academically, musically, athletically, and socially. Cathy was the "good child," scared of violating maternal expectations. Her father was an alcoholic who physically, though not sexually, abused her, then abandoned the family when she was in elementary school. He called every few years at holidays. As adults, they might have dinner together when his work travels would bring him to Cathy's community. Such events were always strained and dishonest.

Previous therapy had focused on these painful events of childhood. During our assessment interview, Cathy revealed that she regularly deceived her family and even her therapists. With family, she created elaborate stories about health problems. At one time her family believed that she had arthritis, which was a fabrication. This justified living away from her family because she needed a "warm and dry" climate. In therapy she simply said what she imagined the therapist wanted her to say. This was a fascinating confession as she entered a new therapeutic relationship with me.

Therapist: What do you think we therapists want to hear?
Cathy: Oh, that I'm feeling better. I'm in control of my anxiety. Things like
               that make therapists feel good.

At the risk of cynicism, I could see that she was a natural politician. She lied easily, but her lies were sly and diplomatic. She measured words so as to ensure that she would not be injured by them at a later time. Unflattering details were omitted. Her political career and her business success were a measure of this tactical skill.

I had difficulty coming up with a diagnosis. Cathy demonstrated aspects of many disorders. She exhibited dissociative episodes, somatic symptoms, depression, and anxiety. Her mental state before each dissociative experience was that of extreme stress and anxiety following conflict in business or politics.

Cathy: Try running a small business when you're up against the megamarts.
               I have employees who depend on my shops to pay their mortgages
               and doctor bills. I stand between them and welfare.

Conflict yielded dissociation. On the day she was arrested for speeding in a neighboring state, she had earlier received a planning commission report granting permission for a national retailer to build near her most profitable boutique. Though legal, she suspected that the permit was being pushed by her political enemies.

With major setbacks in work or politics, a dissociation would follow. Her response to acute stress was anxiety and dissociative "trips." I targeted the stress as the core issue. Once her traffic violations became news fodder, the pressure cooker exploded, prompting a major depressive episode as a differential diagnosis. I sent her back to her psychiatrist to be evaluated for medication to get the anxiety under control while seeing me in short-term therapy.

But I knew there was so much more. During the initial session Cathy described the state of her marriage.

Cathy: In spite of all that has happened, the legal mess, the job, the loss of
               friends, in spite of everything, our marriage has never been stronger.
               We've become so much closer through all of this.

Peculiar! I could not imagine how losing my driver's license would improve my marriage!

Cathy's life story offered clues. She feigned illness to gain the attention of her very busy mother. Even her father was compassionate when she was ill. I began to think of her broader relational needs. How does she maintain relationships with those whom she loves? What does she need to do to get confirmation from others that she is valued and loved? I decided to ask her to invite her husband to attend a few sessions, and he came to the third session.

Thomas was a bit reserved and cautious at first, but he showed willingness to participate. He described himself as scared, exhausted, and frustrated with his wife's recent misbehavior. He was like a lost child at the supermarket, desperately worried about his current plight, yet trying with all of his might to hold on to his objectivity and resourcefulness.

Thomas had been married and divorced once before. He was a dentist in a small solo practice and was content with his career. His motive to please others was strong, as was his resentment when he felt used. He, like Cathy, came from a family of abuse and alcoholism. Rage was the language of his childhood home. He learned how to preempt the explosions of both parents by anticipating all that might anger them and fixing it. If an older sibling neglected to wash the dishes in the morning, Thomas would do it himself, sparing himself his mother's anger should she discover a chore uncompleted. Staying home sick meant that his father would have to stay with him and miss a day of work. Rather than catch that rage, Thomas went to school sick only to be sent home by the school nurse. That strategy diminished his father's wrath. Thomas learned to deny his needs to avoid conflict with his parents, while Cathy exaggerated her needs to gain parental affection.

Marital conflict erupted from Thomas's desire to have time alone in the evening. He cherished sitting in the basement den reading or listening to music. Cathy, on the other hand, "always wants us to be together and would feel neglected if we are not talking." I heard in his story an approach–avoidance pattern. He was the "resentful caretaker." He found satisfaction in helping and supporting but didn't want help for himself. A life theme appeared to be: "Because I have been good and helped you when you were needy, you should not make demands upon me."

Cathy and Thomas both feared rejection and abandonment and had limited capacities to trust. Each constructed complicated mechanisms of behavior to provide the basic relational sustenance for survival. Cathy tried to control the considerable anxiety generated by her business and political work. Dissociation and depression were side effects. I wanted to untangle the roots of her long-standing relational patterns.

Thomas responded to his need for love and safety by becoming the caregiver. Attributing his professional and personal motivation to that dreaded pathological syndrome called "middle-child," he developed a successful routine of attending to others and resisted efforts by others to understand and offer aid for his own pain.

Together, Thomas and Cathy presented a healthy front. In public, they laughed easily at each others' foibles. The private reality of anger and resentment was covered by this gauze of public performance. Thomas retreated into himself and his basement den easy chair and compact disc player. Cathy submerged herself in work and community responsibility. In session, Thomas complained of exhaustion and betrayal. He had loyal intentions but was unaware of limits and boundaries. He identified feelings of resentment, saying he was "constantly attending to her needs and feeling guilty when I just want to be alone."

Cathy bemoaned loneliness, isolation, and disregard.

Cathy: I want to know that you care for me, and I want to know who you are. You are great at fixing things! I feel like I am married to the Maytag repairman. You sit in the basement and wait for something to break, as though that is your only job. But nobody knows you, especially me!

My conceptual frame was now complete. Cathy's dissociative experience was always present subsequent to identifiable stressors. For Cathy, security and significance in a relationship were to be obtained by being in crisis. With each crisis, she expected someone to step up to the plate and confirm that she was important, cherished, valued, and protected. In the current situation, Cathy's dissociation and subsequent "tours" amplified the crisis and prompted Thomas to act in his caregiving role. His rescues brought stability, but Thomas had his limits. Soon, he felt that too much of the marriage was about Cathy, and he would head for the basement. This, in turn, upset Cathy, and the cycle was ready for another revolution.

▨ Process

I had two "assessment and strategy" sessions with Cathy before inviting Thomas. I dedicated the third session to Thomas and brought the couple together in the fourth session to decide on a course of treatment. I gave them the option of individual therapy for Cathy to address dissociation, anxiety, and depression *or* marital therapy, using the relationship to resolve the symptoms. They chose marital therapy.

The first task was to define the projections or roles exhibited by the couple, and this continued through the seventh week of therapy. The fifth visit began with the following dialogue:

Cathy: This was just a horrible week. I called Sid Adolphus, the assistant to the city manager, to see why I hadn't received budget briefings. We're in the budgeting phase for the next year. Sid said the mayor instructed him not to mail the information to me because of "health reasons." That I was, in essence, taking a leave of absence.

Thomas: (interrupting, with a tone of righteous indignation) This is what Cathy has to deal with every day. Local government is ruthless. They will stab you in the back. They're all moral reptiles.

Cathy: But other than that, our week was pretty good, don't you think so, Dear?

Thomas:	Yeah, we had a pretty good week being consumed with what stunt they would pull next.
Therapist:	Cathy, you were talking about being left out of the loop at city government. Then Thomas jumped in, as if on cue, and you appeared to relax. I had this vision of Thomas playing the "I'll take the bullet" role.
Thomas:	The things that she goes through really affect me.
Therapist:	There may be a pattern here. It reminds me of how you would clean up your sister's messes before your mother found out.
Thomas:	I remember that there was such craziness in my family. Little things would get so out of proportion. My sister's job was to iron my dad's handkerchiefs. One time when he ran out of clean ones, he went ballistic. I hid in my room.
Therapist:	Do you see a pattern?
Thomas:	This situation definitely feels out of control, just like then.

Thomas kept the lid on the family's emotional life. However, his care came with a price to all concerned. Thomas kept his own emotional pain safely to himself. Cathy could not be trusted to hold his heart in her hands. No one could. He would tend to his own wounds and subtly inflict guilt when his withdrawal produced feelings of abandonment in Cathy.

The next week, Thomas, again on cue, became supportively angry on Cathy's behalf. The price, though not clearly articulated, was time alone to care for himself. Resentment emerged when Cathy failed to comply.

Thomas:	I am not sure how much more I can take of Cathy and her demands! I have been there for her, I have bailed her out of jail, I have supported her through this crisis, but when is it going to be my turn! All I want is peace and quiet. I want to be left alone. I want to not have to think about her problems. When I say I need time to myself, she accuses me of withdrawing. I am just exhausted.
Cathy:	Thomas, I want you to be able to have your time and space. All I did was ask you what was going on that you were so quiet, and you exploded.
Therapist:	Cathy, what was your week like?
Cathy:	I thought it was fine until just now. I don't know how he can say those things.
Therapist:	When he does this, how do you usually respond?
Cathy:	There is nothing I can do because he won't let me get near him.

The projections were focusing on the therapeutic screen. Cathy knew how to respond to Thomas by creating crises that would incite him to act. Thomas wanted to be her rescuer but was overwhelmed by the crises. He sought respite through withdrawal. I sympathized with his sadness, anger, and loneliness.

Therapy occurs through understanding and using projections. This is accomplished first by validating the presentation. My empathy for their individual frustration was essential in the formation of trust. I validated Cathy's search for love.

Therapist: I am experiencing you as one who has so longed to have someone
               love you that you were forced to take drastic actions, like pretending
               and creating chaos, in order to obtain that which you so needed.

For Thomas, an example of validation was: "You have cared for others as a way
to ensure that they would never feel the same pain that you have felt."

In the second phase I identify how the current relational styles are useful. I guess
you could call this marital empathy. I affirm that their way of being is reasonable. It may
lack utility, but it is neither stupid nor crazy. This is usually achieved within 8 to 16
weeks of therapy. Cathy caught on first. In Session 10, she described an epiphany.

Cathy: I saw myself doing it this weekend, and I stopped.
Therapist: Tell me what you saw and what you did.
Cathy: On Saturday evening when I got home from the store, Thomas was
               reading in the living room. He had already eaten dinner. I was mak-
               ing a sandwich in the kitchen. I was thinking that Thomas really didn't
               love me because if he did, he would be in the kitchen talking to me. I
               realized that I couldn't say anything about this, or he would get mad.
               I felt pitiful. I wanted to cry because I was all alone. Then I said to
               myself, "Cathy, grow up! This is about a sandwich!"

This was worthy of acknowledgment. We celebrated the birth of a new role!
Cathy had stepped outside of herself and was able to observe and alter the process.
    Both partners were learning to empathize.

Cathy: I understand that all of Thomas's loner behavior is not about him not
               wanting to be with me. I am seeing him as more complicated than
               that.

"Perfect," I thought.
    The final step is to develop new relational skills. At this point my role shifted
from being insight-oriented to being instructional, a coach. This phase took about five
sessions. A key event must occur to prompt the successful transition from the identification of the old relational style to the development of new relational skills. There
must be an invitation from one partner to the other to develop these skills, but each
had to wait. For Thomas to jump in and fix it would be to reenact old patterns.
    Cathy made the significant invitation to Thomas in Session 19.

Cathy: I need to be a direct communicator of my feelings, especially when
               I'm afraid. But if I am honest with you, I face rejection. Will you help
               me face my fears?

During that same grand session, Thomas invited Cathy to attend to his issues.

Thomas: Cathy, I need to talk about my needs, not just yours. I usually just
               avoid acknowledging my problems, but that has to change.

Outcome

I worked with Cathy and Thomas weekly for six months (27 sessions). Cathy's anxiety and depression dissipated. The anxiety and the seductive call to dissociation is still there. She can identify the impulse to flee when faced with an intense challenge. The threat of shame and fear that she will be a failure is just below the surface. But she has a new set of psychological tools. When she feels that "let's check out and go for a drive" feeling, she calls Thomas on the cell phone. This required Cathy to learn the stress cues and body sensations that can predict a dissociative episode. She briefly describes her feelings, and Thomas validates them. The conversation concludes with a statement like, "That is a difficult and complicated problem that sounds horrible right now. I believe that with time you will figure out a way to resolve it." A new role was created. *Support* replaces rescuing.

I see the couple every few months for a progress check. Cathy continues to create opportunities for Thomas to find introverted solace, while he seeks to break out of his protective "psychological basement" and engage in the relationship. Change for Thomas has been hard because of the nature of his relational injury. He feels safe when he moves in secret.

Discussion

Cathy and Thomas represent much of what is spectacular about the human condition and the process of therapy. I think of marriage as a contract to aid in the process of maturation and development of the other. Most couples aren't equipped for this task and find themselves trapped in old relational patterns. That's where therapy comes in. I believe that Cathy and Thomas, with my assistance, were able to demonstrate the power of a relationship as a therapeutic instrument.

Biographical Statement

James N. Sells, Ph.D., is an associate professor of counseling at Northern Illinois University in De Kalb, Illinois. His teaching and research interests are group and marital therapy and counselor training. Jim maintains a part-time practice in family therapy with a particular interest in marital conflict resolution. Recent publications include "A Pilot Study in Marital Group Therapy" (with Giordano and King, *The Family Journal*, 2001); "Purpose, Process & Product: A Case Study in Marital Therapy" (*The Family Journal*, 2001); and "Marital Group Therapy" (in *Theory and Practice of Group Therapy*, Fall and Levitov, editors, 2000). You can reach Jim at jsells@niu.edu.

19

The Boxer and the Cutman: A Metaphor for a Marriage

Albert Valadez

A troubled marriage is behind a presenting problem of depression, as is so often the case. Eventually, Julia tells her husband that if they don't get professional help the marriage is over. Valadez is not optimistic when a spouse enters therapy under threat of divorce. Valadez likes to expose the stories or narratives that explain underlying issues in a marriage. To do so, to tell these stories, he relies on the metaphorical language offered up by the client. One metaphor, in particular, taken from the brutal world of boxing, somehow clarifies this antagonistic relationship.

Julia, a 32-year-old mother and student working part-time as a clothing department store clerk, presented symptoms consistent with subclinical depression. She had trouble with sleeping, weight gain, and feelings of hopelessness regarding her marriage. The night before I was brought into the picture, Julia told her husband, Jake (age 34), that if they did not seek professional help the marriage would be over. She expressed "not knowing" herself anymore and felt like her 8-year marriage to a verbally abusive husband was largely responsible for her state. I agreed to meet with Julia and Jake for an initial screening in order to assess their appropriateness for couples counseling. I was a therapist at the university counseling center, so the sessions were free.

Conceptualization

I feel that I have been successful working with couples who are experiencing basic communication problems. I've also had success in helping couples heal the wounds caused by infidelity. I've taken on disputes about financial problems with good results. My failures with couples have happened in situations when an unwilling participant was coerced into therapy with an "if we don't get help it's over" threat. Needless to say, I was not optimistic about this case with Julia and Jake.

At the university counseling center, I worked from a brief therapy approach and used systemic and psychodynamic principles and interventions. According to the counseling center's policy, students were allowed 16 sessions per academic year, free of charge. I wondered if I would be doing Julia and Jake a disservice by attempting to address some of these complicated issues in such a limited amount of time.

Given my bad experience with partners who have been given an ultimatum, Jake's apparent willingness to participate in therapy was a pleasant surprise. He said that he wanted to make this relationship work and would do whatever it took. I interpreted his willingness to give therapy a try as a positive sign.

When working with couples, I like to use a narrative approach to engage each member and to encourage healthy dialogue when opportunities arise. I want an atmosphere that is conducive to storytelling. The story gives me the context of the conflict. I see a story or narrative as the "stage" upon which underlying issues are played out. I cue the action by asking for real-life examples of how a conflict manifests itself.

I have the couple practice basic communication skills, such as reflective listening and simple paraphrasing. In Jake and Julia's case, these skills were important to develop in order to break a destructive and habitual mode of interaction.

Process

Session 1. I explained the ground rules. I keep secrets and do not see either partner on an individual basis. If physical or substance abuse is a problem, I recommend other interventions instead of or in conjunction with marriage counseling. Suggestions could include Alcoholics Anonymous meetings or anger management courses. When I explained that the goal of therapy is not necessarily to save the relationship, Jake's face dropped in confusion.

Therapist:	Jake, I noticed a perplexed look on your face.
Jake:	I thought that was the whole reason I was here, to save our marriage.
Therapist:	As a result of therapy, your relationship might improve, or you might decide that you could lead healthier lives apart. I'm hoping that whatever decision you make, it will be an informed one.
Jake:	I see.

Session 2. In the second session, I asked each person about his and her family of origin.

Therapist:	Jake, tell me what it was like growing up in your family.
Jake:	My parents had strict rules for all of us.
Therapist:	How many brothers and sisters?
Jake:	Five in all. Two younger brothers and two older sisters. My father spent more time with the boys. He loved boxing, and we would strap on the gloves and spar. My dad always told me, "Don't worry about the head, go for the body blows, and the head will follow the body down to the canvas."
Therapist:	Sounds like your dad was pretty involved with you.
Jake:	Mom was there, too.
Therapist:	How would you describe the relationship between your mother and father?

I learned from Jake that he had a strong identification with his father and wanted his father's approval. Julia's family of origin narrative revealed that she adopted the role of the emotional caretaker at the expense of her own needs.

Session 3. I like to get a sense of each member's perception of the problem.

Therapist:	Julia, why don't you share with Jake what you feel is keeping this relationship from growing?
Julia:	It has a lot to do with how he talks to me.
Therapist:	Tell Jake. I'll just listen for a while.
Julia:	(turns to Jake) You say that I'm fat and lazy. It really hurts when you call me "thunder thighs" and slap me on the backside and sing, "Watch it jiggle, see it wiggle."
Jake:	Julia, you get me so mad. I always apologize afterward. You know I don't mean those things. I call you fat to help keep you motivated to stay on your diet. You always say you want me to help you, right?
Julia:	Not like that.
Jake:	I don't understand. They are just words. It is not like I hit you or anything.

Jake absolved himself of responsibility, blaming Julia for making him mad. Julia expressed herself to Jake in a sheepish manner. When Jake responded, his voice was slightly elevated but there was an apologetic tone that seemed sincere.

Sessions 4–8. I proceeded to help the couple redirect dialogue toward each other.

Therapist:	Julia, You're tentative when you speak to Jake. Why?
Julia:	I'm scared of how Jake is going to react.
Therapist:	Explain that to Jake.
Julia:	Jake, I'm scared of how you will react to my opinions.
Therapist:	Please be more specific.
Julia:	The other day I asked if we could spend more time together by watching a movie this weekend, and you told me that you already spend all of your free time with me. Then you accused me of saying that you never spend any time with me, and that is not what I was trying to say.

I tried to identify not only the verbal reactions but also the affect underlying these responses.

Therapist:	Jake, tell me a little bit about how this therapy thing has been going for you.
Jake:	(sarcastic) I feel like everything is my fault. I don't do anything right. I knew that coming in, though.
Therapist:	What about me. Where do I fit in?
Jake:	Well, you're on her side. I always feel cornered in here. You don't understand what it is like for me. Julia is really good with words, and she can prove a point better than any lawyer. She can be very overpowering.
Therapist:	Is she like a lawyer when you argue?
Jake:	Yes.
Therapist:	And you? How do you defend yourself in an argument with this smart lawyer?
Jake:	Like a cornered witness.

During this emotionally heightened interchange, I intentionally went with Jake's metaphor of the lawyer rather than use Julia's actual name. I thought that this would reduce the anxiety surrounding Jake's feelings of weakness and inferiority in the presence of his wife.

Jake:	I hit back the only way I know how.
Therapist:	How is that?
Jake:	I tell her she is overweight and has huge thighs.
Therapist:	Go for the body, and the head will follow the body to the canvas?
Jake:	Yes.

Jake had never been able to articulate how inferior he felt when he was conversing with Julia. Julia attempted "to save" Jake by saying that it was all OK and that now she understood why he verbally attacked. I pointed out how this savior dynamic might play a role in maintaining an unhealthy cycle.

I directed Julia to say how she believed she had changed during the course of the marriage. Julia was somewhat uncomfortable, as indicated by the tentativeness in her voice.

Julia:	Uh, it is hard to say.
Therapist:	Just take a moment to think—no rush.
Julia:	I know I'm not the same as I was, but I don't think it is necessarily a bad thing.

This was a crossroad. I could confront the resistance and heighten the emotional intensity or acknowledge the difficulty of the therapeutic direction and come back to the topic at a later time. I choose the latter road. I wish I could report that my decision was based on some meaningful criteria, but, in actuality, I just mentally flipped a coin. I felt confident that if this issue was relevant, it would reemerge later in the process.

<u>Session 9.</u> Jake talked about how his father had instilled in him the need to be strong and to prevent women from controlling him. We continued to work with the boxing metaphor to discuss how to fight fair. Jake saw his father as his corner coach urging him to not let his guard down and get sucker punched. I asked Jake where Julia fit into this picture. Jake introduced a useful metaphor of the "cut man."

Jake:	It's weird. She starts out being my opponent, but then she ends up being my cut man.
Therapist:	What is a cut man?
Jake:	Between rounds he is the guy who tries to stop the bleeding. But when she tries to stop the bleeding, it makes me feel guilty because I just finished pounding (looking at Julia) you for a round, and here you are trying to stop my bleeding. I wish she would just let me bleed, but she loves me too much to let that happen.
Therapist:	Maybe your opponent is not who you think it is.
Jake:	You mean maybe it is me.

I instructed Jake to monitor when he was feeling cornered in an argument and Julia to monitor her tendency to save Jake from his own pain. She saw that all she got for this tendency was Jake's resentment. Subsequently, when I asked about the "state of the relationship," both reported improvement.

<u>Session 13.</u> Jake did not understand how he undermined Julia's self-esteem and sense of control. It was not until the two engaged in a genuine conflict in my presence that Jake was able to realize the power of his words. Jake had come into the session angry that he had failed his eye exam for the renewal of his driver's license. He proclaimed that his sight was fine and that the clerk at the Department of Motor Vehicles office was in error. At this point, Julia spoke up.

Julia:	Jake, maybe glasses would be good for you. I'm always having to read the exit signs for you when we . . . (Jake interrupts)

Jake: That's not true. Why do you lie like that? I never ask you to read the signs for me. You tell me what they say because you assume I can't read them.

Julia: After two years of missing exits, I finally just decided to tell you that the exit was coming up so you wouldn't be embarrassed when you missed it.

When Julia spoke these words, the power balance in the relationship had been disrupted. I could sense that Jake was about to attempt to regain control through a verbal attack, so I interrupted and asked Jake to access the feelings he was experiencing at the moment. He disclosed that he felt frightened and humiliated. Julia reached out to Jake (her cut man role). I signaled Julia to refrain and asked him, "What would it mean to you for Julia to reach out and hug you right now?" He responded, "It would confirm that I don't deserve her."

Session 14. Jake walked in with eyeglasses. He exclaimed that he had not realized how his vision had deteriorated. Julia began to sob. Rather than inquire as to what had suddenly upset Julia, I directed Jake to ask her.

Julia: That is exactly how I have felt for the last two years. I hadn't even noticed that I had changed. I used to be confident and was accustomed to people and coworkers showing me respect. For me, having my life "out of focus" has become normal. I just wanted you to love me, and I didn't know how to make that happen.

This session marked a turning point. For Jake, the metaphor of eyesight bridged the gap between the concrete experience of having to get his own vision corrected and the intangible experience of "seeing" Julia's feelings. While Jake continued to successfully inquire as to how Julia felt, he gained confidence in his ability to communicate on an emotional level.

Outcome

Therapy with me was terminated after the 16th session. The couple was able to acknowledge their successes and failures in our work together and decided to continue counseling with a private clinician. I encouraged Jake to get individual therapy to process issues regarding his relationship with his father. I called three months later to check in with the couple. They were still in marriage counseling. Jake expressed his appreciation and disclosed that he was "seeing some things for the first time." Julia acknowledged that there was still more work to be done but that she was hopeful about the marriage.

Discussion

I must confess that as a graduate student, I found it difficult to read cases such as those compiled in this book. The reason was that the dialogue between therapists and clients seemed just too perfect and artificial. I often wondered if the actual therapeutic interactions illustrated were really that smooth. I realized, after experiencing personal marital therapy and working with my own clients, that the textbook-like dialogue and the linear progression of "getting better" is more often the exception than the rule.

In my own experience with marriage counseling, my spouse and I found ourselves moving backward almost as often as forward. As a couple, we made the mistake of gauging success by how well we got along and did not argue. The fact of the matter is that we spent a great deal of time avoiding the issues rather than engaging in important and authentic arguments.

With this case, I wanted to illustrate the complexities of working with couples. With Jake and Julia, the linear relationship between time and therapeutic progress did not exist. There would be moments of insight followed by regressions into old patterns.

There were so many nuances and layers to Jake's feelings of inferiority. Jake's uncomfortable feelings evoked anxiety, and the use of metaphors helped connect the events that were occurring in the here and now to Jake's old wounds. In other words, the metaphors of poor vision and glasses, boxing and the cut man, and lawyers and witnesses helped Jake access feelings that might otherwise have been too anxiety provoking to confront, much less express.

If overdone, the use of metaphor can become a trivial technique. A client might be left wondering, "Why can't this person just say what he means?" I have found that when the metaphor emerges from me rather than the client, there has been less overall success. When the metaphors come from the client, as in this case, I can more effectively use them as a window of opportunity for insight.

My advice for the counselor in training? Don't get discouraged when the process isn't smooth and unidirectional.

Biographical Statement

Albert A. Valadez, Ph.D., is an assistant professor of counseling at the University of Texas at San Antonio. He recently practiced as a staff clinician at the University of Texas at San Antonio Counseling Center. Albert's counseling experience includes working with adults, children, and couples. He conducts research in neuroscience, counseling supervision, and emotional abuse, and he has a growing interest in gender and ethnic studies. Albert is currently investigating the relationship between adult day care centers and their effects on elderly Mexican American women. You can reach Albert at avaladez@utsa.edu.

Index